HELP YOURSELF TO HEALTH—
THE DELICIOUS WAY!

Ever since 1936, when RAW VEGETABLE JUICES first appeared, countless thousands have received the message—and the benefits—of this remarkable volume. Reprinted annually for the past 35 years, Dr. Walker's classic is here available in this *newly revised and expanded version*.

Here are advice and suggestions even more relevant to the ecology-conscious 70's than to the small interested minority of the 30's, 40's and 50's. This is a book for *now*, when the once-prophetic voices of J. I. Rodale and Rachel Carson have finally proven to be too terribly true!

RAW VEGETABLE JUICES

N. W. WALKER, D. Sci.

Compiled under the direction of and endorsed by
R. D. POPE, M.D.

A JOVE BOOK

RAW VEGETABLE JUICES

A Jove Book / published by arrangement with
the author

PRINTING HISTORY
Fourteen previous printings
Jove edition / October 1977
Seventh printing / May 1983

ISBN: 0-515-06127-1

Jove books are published by The Berkley Publishing Group,
200 Madison Avenue, New York, N. Y. 10016.
The words "A JOVE BOOK" and the "J" with sunburst
are trademarks belonging to Jove Publications, Inc.

PRINTED IN THE UNITED STATES OF AMERICA

FOREWORD

I wish to acknowledge my indebtedness to Norman W. Walker, D.Sc., for his untiring cooperation in the preparation of this book.

Dr. Walker has placed at my disposal, without reservation, the results of his experience, experiments and analyses which have made possible the compilation and publication, for the first time in history, of a fairly complete guide of the Therapeutic uses of our more common, everyday vegetables when these are taken in the form of fresh, raw juices.

It is hoped that this will prove to be not only a useful and handy reference guide for all the members of my profession, but will also be of considerable help to those who wish to derive the utmost benefit from the natural foods which God created for the nourishment of Man.

R. D. Pope, M.D.

WHAT'S MISSING IN YOUR BODY?

I KNOW that if I do not drink a sufficient quantity of fresh raw vegetable juices, then as likely as not, my full quota of nourishment-ENZYMES is missing from my body.

How about YOU?

You, and you alone, are responsible for the result of how you nourish your body. The LIFE in your food is what counts.

Your body is composed of billions of microscopic cells. Your very existence depends on them. They need nourishment, LIVE, active nourishment. It depends on YOU, and on YOU ALONE, whether the food you eat results in nutrition or MALnutrition!

ENZYMES

The basic key to the efficacy of nourishing your body is the LIFE which is present in your food and of those intangible elements known as ENZYMES.

In other words, the element which enables the body to be nourished and to LIVE, that element which is hidden within the seeds of plants and in the sprouting and growth of plants, is a LIFE PRINCIPLE known as EN-ZYMES.

ENZYMES have been described as complex substances which enable us to digest food and to absorb it into our blood. It has also been claimed that Enzymes digest cancers. In order to perform such classified operations, Enzymes would require a body of some kind, a physical or material organism. This they do not have, any more than electricity, with its multitude of phases, such as voltage, amperage, wattage, etc., has substance, but it activates substances of which it is not an integral part. Thus ENZYMES are not "substances." ENZYMES are an intangible, magnetic, Cosmic Energy of Life Principle (not a substance) which is intimately involved in the action and activity of every atom in the human body, in vegetation, and in every form of life.

Once we get this clearly into our consciousness we will know definitely why our food should be intelligently and properly selected, why most of it should be RAW, uncooked and unprocessed.

We cannot have life and death at one and the same time, either in connection with our body, or with vegetables, fruits, nuts and seeds. Where there is LIFE, there are ENZYMES.

ENZYMES are sensitive to temperatures above 118°F. Above 120° ENZYMES become sluggish, just as the human body becomes languid and relaxed in a hot bath. At 130°F the life of ENZYMES is extinct. They are dead.

Within seeds ENZYMES are in a dormant state and, under proper conditions, will remain in a state of suspended animation for hundreds and thousands of years.

As a matter of fact, carcasses of prehistoric animals found in the Northernmost regions of the earth, in Siberia and other glacial regions where they were instantly frozen by cataclysmic ice formations some 50,000 years ago, have been found to contain ENZYMES in abundance, which became active when the flesh was thawed to body temperature. Thus ENZYMES can be preserved at any desired low temperature without loss.

Life, as L I F E , cannot be explained, so we describe ENZYMES as a Cosmic Energy PRINCIPLE or vibration which promotes a chemical action or change in

8

atoms and molecules, causing a reaction, without, however, the ENZYMES themselves changing, being destroyed or used up in the process.

In other words, ENZYMES are catalysts and, as such, they promote action or change without altering or changing their own status.

With this brief explanation you are better able to appreciate the value, the reason, the logic and the intelligence of choosing the food with which you intend to nourish your body, not only food in the RAW state, but also food used and prepared so that it will nourish the cells and tissues of your body in the speediest and most efficient manner possible.

The great Law of Life is REPLENISHMENT. If we do not eat, we die. Just as surely, if we do not eat the kind of food which will nourish the body constructively, we not only die prematurely, but we suffer along the way.

By supplying our body daily with the elements of which it is composed we can have complete health, provided also that we give due thought, attention and consideration to the other two parts of our being, namely, our Mind and our Spirit.

We can eat the finest and most constructive food in creation, but this will not prevent the disintegration of the body if resentments, fear, worry, frustration and negative states of mind are permitted to obsess us.

Health is the indisputable foundation for the satisfaction of life.

Everything of domestic joy or occupational success must be built of body wholesomeness and vitality.

Nutrition must be vital, or ORGANIC, and salts and mineral matter must be vitally organic in order that they may be assimilated by the human body for the rebuilding and regeneration of the body cells and tissues.

The rays of the SUN send billions of atoms into plant life, activating the ENZYMES, and by this force they change INorganic elements into ORGANIC or life-containing elements for food.

Thanks to the researches of Science we are now able to analyze and know exactly the elements which foods carry, and to harmonize them in the body according to its needs.

Our body is made up of many atomic elements,* the principal ones being:

Oxygen	Calcium	Sodium	Chlorine
Carbon	Phosphorus	Magnesium	Fluorine
Hydrogen	Potassium	Iron	Silicon
Nitrogen	Sulphur	Iodine	Manganese

Except in the case of accidents, all the repair and re-generation of our body must come from within. If the blood stream, the cells and tissues, the organs, the glands and all the rest of the body do not contain these elements in their proper proportion, or if any of these elements is deficient, then the body is out of balance and the condition develops which is known as Toxemia, and Toxemia means just plain poison.

In order to regain and to maintain the proper balance of Health, most of the food we eat must contain live, vital, organic elements, and these are found in fresh raw vegetables and fruits, in nuts and in seeds.

Oxygen is one of the most essential elements. As soon as food is cooked its oxygen is lost, the EN-ZYMES are destroyed at 130°F, and most of the vital force needed for nourishment is dissipated.

The fact that for generations millions upon millions of people have lived, and are living, who have rarely if

(*For more complete and instructive details regarding these elements, read DIET & SALAD SUGGESTIONS, by N. W. Walker, D.Sc., published by Norwalk Press.)

ever eaten anything BUT cooked foods, does not prove that their being alive is the result of eating cooked foods. As a matter of fact they are in a state of decadent existence which is confirmed by the toxic condition of their bodies, whether or not they are aware of this. Else WHY the overcrowding of inadequate hospital facilities; why the millions upon millions of pounds of painkillers sold annually; WHY such a high rate of incidence of heart trouble, diabetes, cancer, emphysema, premature senility and premature deaths, etc.?

Our Creator developed the human body with an inherent colossal amount of tolerance for body punishment. When we eat anything that is "not good" for us or that is incompatible with our nutritional requirements and balance, we suffer. We are warned and punished by pain or by cramps, leading eventually to dis-ease and perhaps to any one or more of the infinite number of ailments which afflict humanity.

Such punishment may not manifest itself immediately nor be immediately apparent, but because of the body's miraculous tolerance we will be kept waiting for days, perhaps for months or maybe for years, before the long-range retribution called for by Nature for the infraction of Her Laws catches up with us.

Once we have discovered the Natural means to regain and to maintain our Health at a high rate of vibration, and have experienced the bliss which results from putting that discovery into daily practice, it seems to us both strange and pitiful that so many people will not consider the matter, but will deliberately continue into a slow state of toxemic decadence, when a little study, coupled with mental and intestinal fortitude, could help them avoid premature, and often painful, disintegration.

WHY NOT EAT THE VEGETABLES?

Without the knowledge of the principles involved in the use of fresh raw vegetable and fruit juices, one would naturally ask: "Why not eat the whole vegetables and fruits instead of extracting the JUICE and discarding the fibers?"

The answer is simple: Solid food requires many hours of digestive activity before its nourishment is finally available to the cells and tissues of the body. While the fibers in such food have virtually no nourishing value, they do act as an intestinal broom during the peristaltic activity of the intestines, hence the need to eat raw foods in addition to drinking juices. By the removal of the fibers in the extraction of the juices, however, such juices are very quickly digested and assimilated, sometimes in a matter of minutes, with a minimum of effort and exertion on the part of the digestive system.

It is well known, for example, that CELERY, because of its high sodium chloride content, is our best food to counteract the effects of extreme heat. To eat the celery would involve so much time in the process of digestion that one may readily be overcome by the intense heat before the beneficial effects from the celery can be obtained.

On the other hand, by drinking a glass or a pint of fresh RAW CELERY JUICE we get quick results. This has many a time made sizzling Arizona Desert heat quite bearable for me.

Whole vegetables and fruits are composed of a considerable quantity of fibers. Within the interstices of these fibers are enclosed the atoms and molecules which are the essential nutritional elements which we need. It is these atoms and molecules AND their respective EN-

ZYMES in the fresh raw juices which aid the speedy nourishment of the cells and tissues, the glands, the organs and every part of our body.

The fibers of vegetables and fruits are nonetheless also valuable. When the food we eat is raw, uncooked and unprocessed, these fibers act as an intestinal broom. When such food is cooked, however, the intense heat destroys its life. Its fibers, having lost their magnetism through the heat, being lifeless, dead, act in the nature of a mop swabbing through the intestines, all too often leaving a coating of slime on the walls of the intestines. In course of time this slime accumulates, putrefies and causes Toxemia. The Colon then becomes sluggish and distorted and constipation, colitis, diverticulosis and other disturbances result.

The juices extracted from fresh raw vegetables and fruits are the means by which we can furnish all the cells and tissues of the body with the elements and the nutritional ENZYMES which they need, in the manner in which they can be most readily digested and assimilated.

Notice that I said NUTRITIONAL ENZYMES. This applies to the ENZYMES in our food. The cells and tissues of our body have their own corresponding ENZYMES which assist and cooperate in the work of digesting and assimilating our food. In addition, every atom and molecule composing our body has a superabundant supply of ENZYMES.

The air we breathe, for example, is taken into our lungs as a combination of approximately 20% Oxygen and 80% Nitrogen. The air we expel from our lungs, on the other hand, is mainly carbonic acid and carbon dioxide. What happens to the Nitrogen?

This is what happens when we breathe: Two main classes of ENZYMES in our lungs come into action the moment air reaches the tiny bunch-of-grapes-like interior of our lungs, known as alvioli. One set of ENZYMES, known as Oxidase, separate the Oxygen while the other set of ENZYMES, known as Nitrase, separate the Nitrogen from the air. The Oxygen is collected, also by ENZYME action, by the blood and circulates it in through the body, while the Nitrogen, by the action of "transportation" ENZYMES, passes into the body for protein generation.

In the mouth, in the stomach, in the intestines and through the entire system there are innumerable ENZYMES, more than a dozen of which are involved in the digestion and assimilation of our food, in conjunction and in cooperation with the ENZYMES in the atoms and molecules contained in the food itself.

COOKED FOODS

As a rule it will do no great harm to eat a little cooked food, occasionally, but never fried food, provided that a sufficient quantity of raw food is also eaten. We are now living in the Atomic Age, and to slow ourselves down by eating much cooked food creates a physical and mental conflict within us which is a handicap blocking the stream-line of our existence.

The juices extracted from fresh raw fruits and vegetables form the means of furnishing all the cells in the body with the elements they need, in the manner in which they can be most readily assimilated.

We must bear in mind that while it is true that cooked and processed foods SUSTAIN life, nevertheless that does not mean that they have the power to regenerate the atoms which furnish the life force to our body. On the contrary, progressive degeneration of the cells and tissues follows the continuous consumption of cooked and processed foods.

There is not a drug in the world that will supply the blood stream with anything in a way in which the body can use it for permanent repair or regeneration.

One can eat four or five big meals a day, and yet the body may be starved through the lack of the vital elements in the food and the disturbance of the ENZYME balance.

Fruit juices are the cleansers of the human system, but the fruit should be ripe. An apple a day will keep the doctor away if we also eat plenty of other raw food. But fruits, with only three or four exceptions, should never be eaten during the same meal in which starches and sugars are included. Fruits, in sufficient variety, will furnish the body with all the carbohydrates and sugar that it needs.

Vegetable juices are the builders and regenerators of the body. They contain all the amino acids, minerals, salts, enzymes, and vitamins needed by the human body, provided that they are used fresh, raw, and without preservatives, and that they have been properly extracted from the vegetables.

Like all the most valuable things in life, the vital part of the vegetables—that which contains the greatest concentrated value—is the most difficult to reach, being hidden within the fibers. Hence the need for a thorough mastication of all raw vegetables.

In the final analysis, raw food is the nourishment intended for human beings. However, not everybody is able to change, overnight, so to speak, the life-long habit of eating foods mostly or all cooked and devitalized, and in their place eat all raw foods. Such a sudden change may cause disturbances which the individual may not be able to understand, but which, nevertheless, may be entirely beneficial. Under these circumstances, it is wise to consult someone who is experienced in the reactions which may result from such a change. After all, it does require considerable mental as well as intestinal fortitude to make this change and to stay with it, but we have found that it pays to do so.

In any event, fresh raw vegetable juices are most necessary as a supplement to every kind of diet, even when no special diet is followed and the individual eats anything and everything he pleases.

When a promiscuous unregulated food regimen is followed or indulged in, such juices are truly of most vital importance because they will furnish to the body the LIVE elements and vitamins deficient in the cooked and processed foods.

On the other hand, an entirely raw food regimen, without the inclusion of a sufficient quantity and variety of fresh raw juices, is equally deficient. The reason for this deficiency lies in the fact that a surprisingly large percentage of the atoms making up the nourishment in the raw foods is utilized as fuel for energy by the digestive organs in their processes of digesting and assimilating food, which usually require as long as 3, 4, or 5 hours after every meal. Such atoms, then, while furnishing some nourishment to the body, are mostly used up as fuel, leaving only the smaller percentage available for the regeneration of the cells and tissues.

When we drink raw vegetable juices, however, the situation is entirely different, as these are digested and assimilated within 10 to 15 minutes after we drink them and they are then almost entirely used in the nourishment and regeneration of the cells and tissues, and of the glands and organs of the body. In this case the result is obvious, as the entire process of digestion and assimilation is completed with the maximum degree of speed and efficiency, and the minimum of effort, on the part of the digestive system.

The important thing is to drink your juices fresh, daily, irrespective of the manner or process by which they have been extracted. Naturally, the more completely the juice is extracted, the more efficiently will it do its work in the body.

MY FIRST CARROT JUICE

My first experiments were made by grating carrots on anything that would reduce them to a pulp, then squeezing the pulp in a cloth, to get the juice. After discovering the miracle of using that juice so simply made, I tried making the carrots into pulp by other means until I could make a larger amount of juice for myself in less time and with less effort. I soon discovered that these juices fermented and spoiled unless used immediately, the time element being the factor.

Eventually I discovered a means to triturate the vegetables almost instantly into a pulp nearly as fine as apple butter, thereby splitting open the interstices of the cells of the fibers, liberating the atoms and molecules. Then, by squeezing the pulp in a hydraulic press I obtained a virtually complete extraction of the juice, and its quality was unsurpassed.

Such a triturator and hydraulic press is naturally expensive equipment. However, do not consider the expense involved, but rather the investment in health that pays for itself!

The centrifugal type of juicer which came on the market some years ago has been much improved over the years and there are some very satisfactory ones now on the market. These have their place in the extraction

17

of juices, in that they are suitable for travel and also for use in small apartments where space is limited. The juices made with this type of equipment have been used with benefit by many people. We need to drink juices daily, irrespective of how they are extracted. However, the best quality of juice is the cheapest in the long run and the most effective in nourishing the body.

Any fresh raw juice is better than no juice at all.

The juice extracted by the centrifugal method should be used immediately, because unless the extraction of the juice from the fibers is as complete as it is humanly and mechanically possible to achieve, oxidation and heat from friction will tend to spoil the juice in a short time.

In my experiments I have found that the toxic sprays are retained in the fibers of vegetables and are not present in the fiber-free juices.

JUICES ARE NOT CONCENTRATED FOOD

Our Creator gave us food both as nourishment and as medicine. It is only natural, therefore, to use our food with both these goals in view.

It is foolish to say that juices are a concentrated food. Nothing could be farther from the truth. A concentrated food is a product which has been dehydrated, from which its water content has been dissipated. Juices, on the other hand, are very liquid food, mostly organic water of the finest quality, with the nourishing atoms and molecules in comparatively microscopic volume. It is this microscopic volume for which the cells and tissues of the body are starved!

In the extraction of "complete" juices, it is essential that the fibers be properly triturated,* in order that the vital elements may be released into the liquid.

It has been demonstrated by the researches of this author, one of the pioneers in the reduction of raw vegetables into their liquid form, that the fibers must be properly triturated to begin with. The juice must then be expressed from the resultant pulp by a hydraulic or equivalent pressure. Otherwise, the vitamins, the enzymes, and the entire volume of vital elements of the vegetables are not likely to be found in the juice.

When so extracted, however, the raw vegetable juices are readily and quickly assimilated by the human body and, being an organic or live food, they regenerate the entire body with surprisingly rapid results.

Under no circumstances consider that fresh raw vegetable juices are a concentrated food or medicine when they are in their natural state. As a matter of fact, they are among the least concentrated and yet the most nourishing of our foods.

To dispel such nonsense about the concentrated quality of these juices, just consider how much more concentrated than the juices are the following items used as food: Soy bean and soy bean flour are 870% more concentrated than carrot juice and 940% more than celery juice. Popcorn is 2100% more concentrated than carrot juice and 2300% more than celery juice. White sugar is 4200% more concentrated than carrot juice and 4600% more than celery juice.

When we realize how colossal is the concentration of these items used as food compared to those juices, we get an inkling of the underlying cause of the acidity generated in the body as a result of eating soy products, popcorn, sugar, and the like.

(*Triturating means ripping open the cells of the fibers of vegetables and fruits.)

If a more convincing fact were needed to dispel the false assertion that these juices are dangerous because concentrated or for any other reason, compare carrot juice, for example, to fresh, undiluted cow's milk, and we find that in their natural chemical composition the water content of these two products is almost identical in volume. The relative natural water content is the basis upon which the concentration of a product is established.

Of course, to compare cow's milk in any way to carrot juice is decidedly paradoxical. Cow's milk is probably the most mucus-forming food used by human beings. The casein content of cow's milk is exceedingly high, being about 300% more than is contained in mother's milk. (Casein, by the way, is a milk by-product used as one of the most tenacious adhesive glues for gluing wood together.) This is one of the reasons for the mucous condition of children and adults brought up to drink quantities of such milk and for the resultant colds, running noses, tonsil, adenoid, and bronchial troubles—whereas carrot juice is one of the greatest aids in the elimination of mucus!

This prodigious generation of mucus in the body as a result of drinking such quantities of cow's milk is not limited to youngsters but is found just as much in adults, where the effects are likely to be far more disastrous because, as people grow older, their resiliency is correspondingly lower than in the younger generation.

When milk is needed, there is one kind of milk that is compatible with human digestion from infancy to senility, and that is RAW GOAT'S milk.

Raw Goat's milk is not mucus forming. If a mucous condition develops after drinking it, it will usually be due to an excessive previous use of starches and sugars, but not to the Goat's milk. This milk must be used

20

RAW, however, and it must not be heated above 118°F, nor pasturized.

For infants there is no better milk than mother's milk. Raw Goat's milk is the next best. Some fresh raw carrot juice may be added to it with benefit. In fact, Raw Goat's milk can be added to any fresh raw vegetable juices satisfactorily. We will have more to say about MILK, later.

We must always bear in mind that, in the use of fresh raw vegetable and fruit juices, the QUALITY of the juices has a distinct bearing on the results obtained.

When the juices are incompletely extracted from the vegetables or from the fruits, they are in the form of vital organic water and as such are still beneficial, but their effective power is proportionately diminished due to the absence of the vitamins and enzymes which are left behind in the fiber and the pulp.

The various members and organs of the human body, as well as every part comprising them, are composed of microscopic cells containing the various elements already listed. These cells are constantly being used up in the normal course of human existence and must be constantly rebuilt. The food required for this purpose must be vital organic food and must contain an ample supply of the vital organic minerals and salts needed for the efficient upkeep of the system.

A diet consisting wholly or mainly of devitalized foods inevitably results in the breaking down of these cells, creating a condition of sickness, or disease.

To avoid such a condition it is necessary to furnish the body with an abundance of vital elements in its nutrition. When the breaking down of these cells is taking, or has taken, place, then the natural way to return to normal would be to thoroughly cleanse the system and

21

start a process of reconstruction by means of raw vegetable juices.

It has been proved beyond doubt that supplementing our meals with raw vegetable and fruit juices is the quickest and most permanent way to replenish the body with the elements it lacks, and the following will be found useful as a guide in the use of such juices, when properly extracted.

HOW WE PROTECT OURSELVES AGAINST PESTICIDES AND SPRAYS IN THIS POISONED WORLD

There is a little known fact regarding the effect of pesticides on our vegetables and fruits, which should be given much publicity in these times.

We have been able to determine that, whereas pesticides and sprays may be injurious in the consumption of vegetables and fruits, it is the FIBERS of such foods that collect these toxins. The enzymes, atoms and molecules are allergic to them.

It is axiomatic and well known that the contributing factor in the deficiency of, or lack of balance in the elements in natural food products is in direct relation to the corresponding deficiency or lack in the soil in which such products were grown.

If the soil in which vegetables and fruits are grown is devitalized to any extent by lack of or by improper composting and/or fertilizing, whatever products are grown in that soil will be deficient in vital factors in direct proportion to the deficiency or lack of the nutrient factors in that soil.

Furthermore, under the very best soil conditions, the use of sprays and pesticides will enter into the plants and roots, but will be completely absorbed by the fibers of such plants and such roots. The plants will continue to grow and thrive, not because of these toxins, but in spite of them. Why? Because the enzymes, atoms and molecules will continue to carry on their work without interruption, in spite of the poison-saturated fibers.

The question, then, arises: How to get the enzymes, atoms and molecules from our vegetables without using the poisoned fibers? After all, these enzymes, atoms and molecules are the nourishing elements we require. The fibers have virtually no nourishing value.

The answer is simple: By the process of triturating the vegetables, the cells of the fibers are split open and these elements are released. The result is a pulp almost as fine as apple butter. These elements are just as allergic to toxins as oil is to water. They will therefore retain their virgin virtue by not mixing integrally with the triturated fibers.

By squeezing this triturated pulp through proper straining material the juice, containing all the enzymes, atoms and molecules, is extracted free from the fibers and the toxins with which they are saturated.

Here, therefore, we have found our answer on how to avoid being afflicted by the pollution which has infested food products throughout our Nation.

Our use of the electric triturator and hydraulic press, however, does not rule out the use of centrifugal machines. While it is recognized that by centrifugal action we cannot extract ALL of the enzymes, atoms and molecules, nevertheless by the use of a filter in the centrifugal extractor the filter prevents the fibers from mixing with the extracted juice. We can thus obtain a juice which is free from the poison-saturated fibers.

The appliance known as a Liquefier or Blender is not practical for the extraction of juices. Its action merely cuts up the vegetables as fine as desired, but the pulp is still present in its entirety.

We use these Blenders in our kitchen to make dressings, desserts, etc., for which purpose they are admirably suited.

In our choice of vegetables and other foods, we shop at whatever market or Supermarket has the freshest and best quality vegetables and other foods, and at the Health Food Stores. We always shop for QUALITY. There is no substitute for QUALITY, at any price, and if the cost is higher, it is both safer and more economical in the long run.

When we eat Salads, it would be ridiculous and useless to try to separate the elements from the fibers. We therefore apply for security from the effects of any toxins which may be lurking in such food, by contacting the highest source possible, our Creator, Almighty God, asking His Blessings on it, and His Blessings have never yet failed to protect us.

Furthermore, our Blessings have been multiplied beyond what we think we deserve, besides having the vibrations of our food raised to their highest nutritional point. It is the Hand of Almighty God that guides us in our discoveries. We pass them on to you.

HOW MUCH JUICE
CAN BE TAKEN SAFELY?

Just as much as one can drink comfortably without forcing oneself. As a general rule one pint daily is the least that will show any perceptible results and preferably from two to eight pints or more. We must bear in mind that the more juice we drink the quicker will be the results.

When juices were first promulgated from the lecture platform, it was suggested that they be taken in small doses. This was undoubtedly due to the fact that there was no machine on the market at the time with which juices could be made in reasonable quantities. To make even a cupful of juice at a time with a hand juicer was difficult and laborious. Had larger quantities of juice been advocated, then, undoubtedly, there would have been little market for hand juicers because of the labor involved in using them. Today we find the electric Triturator and Hydraulic Press HOME JUICER the most efficient.

There are certain definite principles involved, first, in releasing the mineral and chemical elements and the vitamins and hormones from the tiny microscopic cells of the fibers of vegetables and fruits, and second, in collecting them and separating them and the juice from the fiber.

No practical hand juicer has been found by us that can possibly extract all of the vital elements from the vegetables, as they only partly crush the fibers but do not triturate them, and trituration is the fundamental principle, discovered by the Norwalk Laboratory of Nutritional Chemistry and Scientific Research, in the liberation and reclamation of these vital elements.

Howbeit, centrifugal and other such machines are just as useful when the supreme quality of the juices is not of paramount importance. Furthermore, such machines do not involve the large investment of money required for a Triturator and Hydraulic Press.

The principle of the centrifugal type of juice extractor involves a fast rotating plate with a sharp grating surface at the bottom of the basket in the machine. As the rotation is extremely fast, the pulp which is grated on the bottom plate is flung by centrifugal force against

25

the sides of the perforated basket and the juice from the pulp is thus separated and collected through a spout.

Of course it is understandable that it is physically and mechanically impossible to extract ALL of the juice by centrifugal action, but the juice so obtained is generally good and should not be kept long before drinking it.

Notwithstanding the disadvantages of such methods of extraction, however, there is still much benefit derived from drinking such juices. The inherent natural water in such juices is, after all, ORGANIC water and as such it has great value. Such vitamins and mineral elements as are collected in such juice are very beneficial.

When we speak of WATER, the first thought is quite naturally of that which comes from the faucet or from the spring, or even rain water. Few people stop to wonder if, or even to realize that, there is vital ORGANIC as well as INORGANIC water. Nature has furnished vegetation as the laboratory in which to convert the inorganic water of rain and stream into life-containing atoms of vital organic water. The water from the faucet is not only inorganic, the atoms composing it being mineral elements entirely devoid of the life principle, but nearly all cities contaminate the water supply with inorganic chlorine and other chemicals, making it truly unfit for human or animal consumption. The water in the rivers and streams and from the spring is also inorganic, as is rain water.

The only source from which vital organic water is derived is vegetation—our vegetables and fruits and particularly the juices made from these. Such juices, however, must be raw to retain their vital organic quality and must not be cooked, processed, canned, or pasteurized.

When juices have been cooked, processed, canned, or pasteurized, all of the enzymes are destroyed and the atoms are then converted into inorganic or dead atoms; and this applies to the H_2O (water) as well as to the mineral and chemical atoms composing such juice.

To convert vegetables into liquid or semi-liquid mush without eliminating the cellulose is also of little value from the point of view of juices. The very purpose of drinking juices is to enable the body to assimilate all of the vital elements contained in the vegetables or fruits in the quickest possible time and manner, without in any way burdening the digestive organs with the work entailed by the presence of the pulp-cellulose.

Drinking juices which are properly made will enable the body to assimilate them within ten to fifteen minutes; whereas the presence of pulp in the so-called liquid, or liquefied, vegetables, or juices still containing the pulp, will require hours to digest.

Furthermore, to drink juices from which the pulp has not been extracted, taxes the digestive organs more than eating and properly masticating the raw vegetables and fruits themselves, as proper insalivation and thorough mastication is essential to the complete digestion of vegetables when the cellulose fiber is present. This is not usually done if the fibers still remain a part of the mush or liquefied vegetables; whereas, the juices from which the fiber has been removed furnish, without interference, every particle of the nourishment contained in the vegetable for immediate and quick assimilation by the body.

Vegetable juices will contain all of the vital elements, that is to say, all of the vitamins and vital organic minerals and salts contained in the vegetable, if the juices are properly made by means of a thorough trituration or grinding, which will rip open the fibers in the vegetable and reduce the entire vegetables to a pulp so fine that it can be spread almost like apple butter. By placing this pulp in a filter cloth and squeezing it in a hydraulic or similar press—which need not be any larger than can be conveniently handled on a kitchen table—exercising many tons of pressure, we then get a juice which, in comparison with that made inefficiently, is as different as cream from milk.

ALFALFA

ALFALFA is a particularly valuable leguminous herb, not only rich in the principal mineral and chemical elements in the constitution of the human body, but it also has many of the trace elements obtained from deep in the soil where the roots reach down 30 to 100 feet.

Of specific value I would point out the rich quality, quantity and proper balance of Calcium, Magnesium, Phosphorus, Chlorine, Sodium, Potassium and Silicon in Alfalfa. These elements are all very much needed for the proper function of the various organs in the body.

While Alfalfa is widely used as forage for livestock, it is nevertheless of immense value, in the form of juice, using only the leaves, when it can be obtained fresh. It is also known as Lucerne grass, while in England it is known as Purple Medic.

Because Alfalfa adapts itself to widely varying conditions of soil and climate, even thriving on alkali soil, there is no excuse for not growing it on one's home grounds, as it is usually difficult to obtain when living in the City.

When we are unable to obtain fresh Alfalfa, we sprout Alfalfa seeds and eat the sprouts with our meals. They sprout easily and they are very beneficial.

ALFALFA JUICE

Vegetation miraculously transforms and vitalizes inanimate substances into living cells and tissues.

Cattle eat vegetation, raw, for nourishment. They take into their system one living organism and convert it into a still more complex live organism.

Vegetation, on the other hand, whether vegetable, fruit, plant, or grass, takes inorganic elements from the air, from the water, and from the earth, converting them into live organic elements. It takes nitrogen and carbon from the air; nitrogen, minerals, and mineral salts from the earth in which it grows; and oxygen and hydrogen from water.

The most vital and potent factors in this process of conversion are the enzymes and the life-giving influence of the rays of the sun which generate the chlorophyll.

The chlorophyll molecule is made up of a web of carbon, hydrogen, nitrogen, and oxygen atoms around one single atom of magnesium. It is interesting to compare this design with that of the hemoglobin of our red blood corpuscles, which has a similar web of elements girdling an atom of iron instead of the atom of magnesium.

We find in this analogy one of the secrets of the value of chlorophyll to the human system. Strict vegetarians —whose diet excludes grains and starches but includes an abundance of fresh juices with a good proportion of the green juices, are healthier, live longer and are more free from degenerative ailments than those who eat mostly cooked foods and little or no raw vegetables and juices. It would seem that we have here fairly conclusive evidence as to which diet regimen is the correct or natural one for healthy human beings.

One of the richest chlorophyll foods we have is alfalfa. It is a food that builds up both animals and humans, all things considered, into a healthy, vital, and vigorous old age, and builds up a resistance to infection that is almost phenomenal.

The juice of fresh alfalfa is too strong and potent to be taken by itself. It is best taken with carrot juice, in which combination the individual benefits of each juice are intensified. It has been found very helpful in most troubles with the arteries and disfunctions connected with the heart.

It is generally conceded by those who have studied the effects of gas in the intestines that in a surprisingly large number of patients suffering from heart trouble this heart condition is caused not by any organic disfunction of the heart but from excessive gas in the colon pressing the walls of the colon against organs connected with the heart. A few colonic irrigations or high enemas as a rule have frequently relieved this condition. The heart trouble disappeared until the next accumulation of gas gave warning that the colon, not the heart, needed a thorough reconditioning.

Besides benefit to blood and heart conditions, chlorophyll is most useful in the relief of respiratory troubles and discomforts, particularly in the sinuses and in the lungs. Mucus is the underlying cause of sinus infection and pains, as it is of bronchial and asthmatic conditions, including hay fever.

Strict vegetarians who eschew cow's milk, flour, grain, and concentrated sugar products, are not afflicted with these troubles, particularly if they were brought up from childhood to shun and avoid these foods. This is not by any manner or means fanatical. It is just plain common sense and perfectly natural, and proved beyond question or doubt from experience.

Those who have adopted such a vegetarian program

later in life have been able to help overcome these conditions without the use of surgery or drugs.

After all, sinus infection is the work of our defensive friends, the germs, trying to help us by breaking up mucus accumulations so that these may be eliminated from the system. Instead of helping them by cleansing the body of the waste matter by means of colonics and enemas, attempts are made to "dry up" the mucus and "shrink the membranes" with applications of adrenalin, epinephrine, or other drugs. Even "sulfa" drugs, now known to be virulent and pernicious, are sometimes used, without regard to, consideration, or understanding of the eventual damage, injury or danger resulting from their use.

The most injurious results are essentially developed when the waste matter, consisting particularly of these drugs and of the sewage of the germ colonies, are allowed to remain in the "infected" and adjacent parts instead of being eliminated as quickly as possible.

We have in our body the most perfect systems of elimination if we will but get them into efficient working condition.

Our lungs must be free of foul air, tobacco smoke, etc.; our skin must be active so that the pores may pour out the toxins carried there by the lymph; the kidneys must have freedom of action without interference from alcohol and uric acid products; and our colon must have whatever internal washing it needs to remove the accumulations of 30, 40, and 50 years or more.

That is only part of the program, however. The cells and tissues of the entire body must get live organic nourishment. This means that, for some time at least, we should forgo as much as possible all those foods whose vital energy—whose life element—has been destroyed by heat or by processing. We may be guided by

the contents of my book DIET & SALAD SUGGES-
TIONS, which has brought innumerable commenda-
tions from readers who have benefited by putting into
practice the very simple rules and menus contained
therein.

To carrot and alfalfa juice, lettuce juice may be
added to enrich the combination with elements particularly needed by the roots of the hair. Drinking this combination daily, one pint a day, may help the growth of
hair to a remarkable extent.

ASPARAGUS JUICE

Asparagus contains an alkaloid known as Asparagine
in a relatively large amount. (Alkaloids are found in living plants. They contain the active life principle of the
plant, without which it cannot grow or stay alive.) It is
composed of the elements carbon, hydrogen, nitrogen,
and oxygen.

When asparagus is cooked or canned, the value of
this alkaloid is lost, as the hydrogen and oxygen are dissipated and the natural salts formed by the combination
of this alkaloid with the other elements are virtually lost
or their value is destroyed.

In the form of juices asparagus has been very effectively used as a diuretic, particularly when combined
with some carrot juice, as it may prove to be uncom-
fortably strong in its reaction on the kidneys when
taken alone.

It is a beneficial juice in the case of kidney disfunctions and in the regulation of general glandular troubles.
Diabetes and anemia are helped by the use of it in conjunction with the juices more specifically outlined for
these conditions.

As this juice helps the breaking up of oxalic acid

crystals in the kidneys and throughout the muscular system, it is good for rheumatism, neuritis, etc. Rheumatism results from the end product of the digestion of meat and meat products, which generate excessive amounts of urea.

As the human system cannot completely digest and assimilate so-called "complete proteins," such as meats and meat products, the ingestion of too much of these causes the greater part of the uric acid generated thereby to be absorbed into the muscles.

The continuous use of meat protein taxes the workings of the kidneys and of other eliminative organs, straining them to the point where a progressively smaller amount of uric acid is eliminated and a correspondingly greater amount is absorbed by the muscles. The result is painfully known as rheumatism.

This condition is also one of the underlying causes for prostate gland trouble, in which case this juice combination, in addition to the carrot, beet, and cucumber juice has been helpful.

BEET JUICES

This is one of the most valuable juices for helping to build up the red corpuscles of the blood and tone up the blood generally. Women, particularly, have been benefited by drinking at least one pint of a combination of carrot and beet juice daily. The proportion in this combination may vary from 3 to 8 ounces of beet juice, using roots and tops, in one pint of the combined juices, carrot and beet.

Taken alone, beet juice, in greater quantities than a wineglass at a time, may cause a cleansing reaction which may make one a little dizzy or nauseated. This may be the result of its cleansing effect on the liver and may, therefore, be uncomfortable. It has been found from experience that it is best to take less beet juice and more carrot juice in the beginning until one can tolerate its beneficial cleansing effect—then to increase the proportion of beet juice gradually. One 6- or 8-ounce glassful twice daily is usually considered sufficient.

For menstrual disturbances beet juice has been very helpful, particularly when, during such periods, it has been used in small quantities, not more than a wineglass at a time (say, 2 or 3 ounces) two or three times a day. During menopause this procedure has been found much more permanently helpful than the degenerative effects of drugs or of synthetic hormones. After all, any drug or inorganic synthetic chemical product cannot possibly have any more than a temporary effect in giving relief; the one who takes such drugs or synthetic hormones is the one who may suffer eventually when the body and Nature combine in attempts to eliminate such inorganic material from the system. Any drug that can be guaranteed to relieve or cure permanently any sick condition of the body can also be guaranteed to start some other and probably more serious condition some time later. It is the one who takes the drug that suffers in the long run, not those who advertise or administer it.

After all is said and done, Nature has furnished us with natural means through which we may seek health, energy, vigor, and vitality. She has also furnished us, in greater or lesser degrees, with intelligence with which to pursue our search for knowledge. If we use our intelligence, Nature smiles on us. If we do not use it, she stands by with infinite patience and compassion, wondering why her handiwork should turn out to be so stupid.

While the actual content of iron in red beets is not high, it is, nevertheless, of a quality that furnishes excellent food for the red corpuscles of the blood. The great-

34

est virtue of the chemical elements in the beet is the fact that more than 50% is sodium, while the calcium content is only about 5%. This is a valuable proportion for maintaining the solubility of calcium, particularly when, as a result of eating cooked foods, inorganic calcium has been permitted to accumulate in the system and has formed deposits within the blood vessels, resulting in a toughening of the walls, as in the case of varicose veins and hardening of the arteries, or a thickening of the blood, resulting in high blood pressure and other forms of heart trouble.

The 20% potassium content furnishes the general nourishment for all the physiological functions of the body, while the 8% content of chlorine furnishes a splendid organic cleanser of the liver, kidneys, and gall bladder, also stimulating the activity of the lymph throughout the entire body.

The combination of carrot and beet juice furnishes a good percentage of phosphorus and sulphur on the one hand, and potassium and other alkaline elements on the other hand, which together with the high content of Vitamin A, completes what is probably the best natural builder of the blood cells and particularly the red blood corpuscles.

CARROT, BEET AND COCONUT JUICE

With the addition of some pure coconut milk extracted from the meat of the coconut, making a combination of carrot, beet, and coconut juice, a food is obtained which, in addition to its properties as an intensive body builder, has even more potent qualities as a cleanser of the kidneys and gall bladder. If properly prepared, this combination contains the alkaline elements potassium, sodium, calcium, magnesium, and iron in abundance and the other elements phosphorus, sulphur, silicon, and chlorine in ample and correct proportions.

CARROT, BEET AND CUCUMBER JUICE

Gallstones, kidney stones, and gravel in the gall bladder and kidneys are the natural result of the inability of the body functions to eliminate from the system the inorganic calcium deposits formed after eating concentrated starches and sugars.

The gall bladder is directly connected with the liver and with the blood stream by means of the bile duct and the hepatic duct. All the food we eat is "broken down" in the digestive tract, and the elements it contains are carried by the blood to the liver for further processing and segregation. No concentrated grain or flour product can be completely utilized for the reconstruction of cells and tissues, particularly if it has been devitalized by heat. Its component elements, however, must necessarily pass through the liver; and among these elements we have calcium. Such starch molecules are not soluble in water.

Vital organic calcium is needed by the entire system, and such calcium, the only kind that IS soluble in water, can be obtained ONLY from fruits and vegetables, and their juices, when these are raw and fresh. As such, it passes through the liver and is completely assimilated in the process of gland functions and cell and tissue building.

The calcium in all concentrated starches and sugars which have been subjected to heat is inorganic, and is not soluble in water. Its presence in the system is extraneous and foreign, and as such is cast aside at every opportunity by the blood- and lymph-streams. The first convenient dumping ground for it is the bile duct, which carries it to the gall bladder. The next most convenient place is what we may term the dead-ends of blood vessels either in the abdomen, resulting in tumors, or in the anus, resulting in hemorrhoids. Such inorganic calcium atoms as happen to get past these, usually end up in the kidneys.

A few atoms of inorganic calcium, either in the gall bladder or in the kidneys, may not do much harm; but with a continuance of the use of bread, cereals, cakes, and other flour products, the deposits become progressively cumulative and result in the formation of gravel or stones in these organs.

It has been found from long experience that the removal of these deposits or encumbrances by means of surgery is both unnecessary and stupid except, perhaps, in the most extreme cases; and even then, it is doubtful if better results could not be obtained by helping Nature, the Great Healer, by the intelligent use of natural means.

Lemon juice, in the proportion of the juice of one lemon to a tumblerful of hot water, taken many times a day, supplemented with a tumblerful of the combination of carrot, beet, and cucumber juice three or four times a day, has helped a great many sufferers to experience with satisfaction the disappearance of both such gravel and such stones sometimes within a matter of a few days, or a few weeks.

Just to give one instance as an example, we would like to relate the experience of a gentleman well into his forties who was very prominent in the business world, having successfully placed on the highway to fortune several of the large nation-wide chain stores in this country and one or two in Great Britain. For more than 20 years he had suffered acute pains, diagnosed by doctors and hospitals as indicating stones in the gall bladder, confirmed by X-ray pictures taken with and without iodophthalein, the dye used to detect this trouble. Only his fear of, and aversion to, an operation kept his gall bladder where it belonged.

Upon hearing of the success of Juice Therapy and reading one of the earlier editions of this book, he placed himself in the hands of one who was competent from experience to help him, and was told that to give himself a relatively quick treatment with these juices might cause more agonizing pains than any he had suffered before but that these would last a few minutes or, perhaps, an hour or so at a time and would eventually cease altogether with the passing of the dissolved calcium. He drank ten or twelve glasses of hot water with the juice of one lemon in each throughout the day and about three pints of carrot, beet and cucumber juice daily. On the second day he did have some terrific spasms of pain for 10 to 15 minutes each. By the end of the week the crisis arrived and for about half an hour he rolled on the floor in agony; but the pain suddenly left him and a short while afterward stones passed out and caused a reaction like mud in his urine. That evening he was a different man. The next day he took a long trip—from New York to Washington and on to Canada—with me in my car, feeling 20 years younger and marveling at the simplicity of Nature's miracles.

This is not an isolated instance. Thousands the world over have testified with gratitude to the benefits derived from fresh raw vegetable juices.

The combination of carrot, beet, and cucumber juice gives us one of the finest cleansing and healing aids for the gall bladder, the liver, the kidneys, and the prostate and other sex glands.

Something else to bear in mind is the fact that when

we eat meat an excessive amount of uric acid is generated in the system, which apparently cannot be completely eliminated by the kidneys, thus causing a definite strain on these organs, reacting on the rest of the body. This combination of juices is therefore invaluable in this respect to help cleanse the system. At the same time, it has been found advisable to eliminate concentrated sugars and starches, as well as meat, for awhile at least, to give the body the opportunity it needs to readjust itself to normalcy. Once the healthy condition of the body has been re-established, then of course, we should know from experience that to devitalize it again, if we choose to do so, we need only to go back to eating devitalized foods. It is truly gratifying to find that many have no desire to return to a mediocre or worse state of health. They have experienced the realization that health, vigor, energy, and vitality are well worth retaining by the sacrifice of the foods that were more palatable than nourishing.

Nevertheless, nourishing foods are, and can be made, palatable by the simple method of learning how to do it. Study my book DIET & SALAD SUGGESTIONS.

BRUSSELS SPROUTS JUICE

The juice of Brussels sprouts combined with that of carrot, string bean, and lettuce furnishes a combination of elements which helps to strengthen and regenerate the insulin generating properties of the pancreatic functions of our digestive system. For this reason, it has been found of inestimable benefit in cases of diabetes.

This benefit, however, has been derived when all concentrated starches and sugars were avoided altogether and when colonic irrigations and high enemas were used regularly to cleanse waste matter from the system.

CABBAGE JUICE

Duodenal ulcers have responded almost miraculously to the drinking of cabbage juice. The only drawback is the frequent generation of excessive gas. In any case, plain carrot juice has been used with equal success and most people find it more palatable.

Cabbage juice has wonderful cleansing and reducing properties. Sometimes it has a tendency to cause distress because of gas forming in the intestines after drinking it. Such gas is the result of waste putrefactive matter present in the intestines being broken up by the cabbage juice, which causes a chemical reaction to set in and may form gas. This is a natural condition—sulfuretted hydrogen, a foul smelling gas, being the outcome of the cleansing elements in the juice acting on and dissolving the waste matter. Enemas and colonic irrigations help to remove both this excessive gas and the waste matter causing it.

The most valuable properties in cabbage are the high sulphur and chlorine content and the relatively large percentage of iodine. The combination of the sulphur and chlorine causes a cleansing of the mucous membrane of the stomach and intestinal tract, but this only applies when cabbage juice is taken in its raw state without the addition of salt.

When excessive gas or other distress is experienced after drinking raw cabbage juice, either straight or in combination with other raw vegetable juices, it may be an indication of an abnormal toxic condition within the intestinal tract. In such case it has been found advisable, before much of the juice is used, to cleanse the intestines thoroughly by drinking carrot, or carrot and spinach juice daily for two or three weeks and taking enemas, daily. It was found that once the intestines were able to assimilate cabbage juice, it was invaluable as a cleanser, particularly in the case of excessive adipose weight.

When raw cabbage juice is added to raw carrot juice, it forms an excellent source of Vitamin C as a cleansing medium, aiding particularly where infection of the gums is present resulting in pyorrhea. When boiled or dehydrated with excessive heat, however, the effectiveness of the enzymes, vitamins, minerals, and salts is destroyed. One hundred and twenty pounds of cooked or canned cabbage could not furnish the same vital organic food value that is assimilated from drinking one-half pint of straight raw cabbage juice when properly prepared.

Cabbage juice has been used very effectively to help the relief of ulcers and constipation. As constipation is usually the primary cause of skin eruptions, these have also been cleared up with the judicious use of this juice.

The addition of salt to cabbage or its juice not only destroys its value, but is also harmful.

RAW CARROT JUICE

Depending on the condition of the individual, raw carrot juice may be taken indefinitely in any reasonable quantities—from one to six or eight pints a day. It has the effect of helping to normalize the entire system. It is the richest source of Vitamin A which the body can quickly assimilate and contains also an ample supply of Vitamins B, C, D, E, G, and K. It helps to promote the appetite and is an aid to digestion.

It is a valuable aid in the improvement and maintenance of the bone structure of the teeth.

Nursing mothers should drink plenty of raw carrot juice, properly prepared, to enhance the quality of their milk, as a breast milk diet may, under certain circumstances, not provide sufficient vital foods. During the last months of pregnancy, raw carrot juice, taken in sufficient quantities, tends to reduce the possibilities of puerperal sepsis at childbirth. One pint of carrot juice, daily, has more constructive body value than 25 pounds of calcium tablets.

Raw carrot juice is a natural solvent for ulcerous and cancerous conditions. It is a resistant to infections, doing most efficient work in conjunction with the adrenal glands. It helps prevent infections of eyes and of the throat as well as of the tonsils and sinuses and of the respiratory organs generally. It also protects the nervous system and is unequalled for increasing vigor and vitality.

Intestinal and liver diseases are sometimes due to a lack of certain of the elements contained in properly prepared raw carrot juice. When this is the case, then a noticeable cleaning up of the liver may take place, and the material which was clogging it up may be found to dissolve. Frequently this is released so copiously that the intestinal and urinary channels are inadequate to care for this overflow, and in a perfectly natural manner it is passed into the lymph for elimination from the body by means of the pores of the skin. This material has a distinctly orange or yellow pigment and while it is being so eliminated from the body will sometimes discolor the skin. Whenever such a discoloration takes place after drinking carrot or other juices, it is an indication that the liver is getting a well-needed cleansing.

It is NOT the carrot juice itself nor the carotene that comes through the skin, as this discoloration will take place even if the juice is filtered to the point of clearing it of all color pigment. It is just as practical an impossibility for the carrot pigment itself to come through the skin as it would be for the red pigment of the beet to turn the body red or the chlorophyll of the green vegetables to paint the skin green from within.

In any case, is it not better to have a healthy satinlike skin, even though it may be slightly on the carrot shade, than to have the pasty complexion which, together with its pimples and other blemishes, publicizes the unhealthy condition of the body?

Instead of becoming distressed over the appearance of skin discoloration, which will, in any case, eventually disappear, we should be gratified that the disintegration of the liver has been stopped or prevented by the use of these juices.

This discoloration, however, can be somewhat retarded by slowing up the process of cleansing by changing or adding other juices to the particular one that causes such a rapid cleansing activity.

The lack of sufficient rest, sleep and overwork may also result in a certain amount of skin discoloration.

The endocrine glands, especially the adrenals and the gonads, require food elements found in raw carrot juice. Sterility is sometimes overcome by its use. The cause of sterility has been traced to the continuous use of foods in which atoms and enzymes were destroyed by cooking or pasteurizing.

Dry skin, dermatitis, and other skin blemishes are due to a deficiency in the body of some of these food elements contained in carrot juice. This is also a factor in eye trouble, as in ophthalmia, conjunctivitis, etc.

If properly extracted from fresh, clean, good quality raw carrots, this juice is very rich in the vital organic alkaline elements sodium and potassium. It also contains a good supply of calcium, magnesium, and iron; while the vital organic elements phosphorus, sulphur, silicon, and chlorine balance perfectly with the former in their action and reaction on the human system.

43

As an aid to dissolve ulcers and cancer, raw carrot juice has proved itself the miracle of the age. It was found essential, however, that it be properly prepared and every vestige of concentrated sugar, starch and flour of every kind be completely eliminated from the diet.

One of the most insidious causes of ulcers and cancer has been discovered in the victim's nursing resentments for a long time, all too often ever since childhood. Unless resentments are completely dissolved, they can frustrate otherwise most effective attempts to help the patient.

It sometimes happens after drinking large quantities of carrot juice that a reaction is experienced or, perhaps, some distress. This is a perfectly natural sequence as it is an indication that Nature has started house cleaning in the body and that this juice is the most needed implement for this purpose.

To jump to the conclusion that the juice does not agree with one shows lack of understanding, as carrot juice is nothing more nor less than the very finest quality of organic water and the kind of nourishment that the body needs. If the juice is fresh and has been properly made, there is nothing whatever, even by the wildest stretch of the imagination, that can do other than furnish the enzymes, vital atoms, and the vital organic water which the starved body cells and tissues crave and call for.

The addition of some raw goat's milk or a little pure raw cream to the carrot juice gives it a somewhat exotic flavor and often serves to relieve the monotony when a reaction or distress may have a tendency to turn us against the plain juice.

It is pertinent here to remark that cream is a fat, purely and simply, while milk is definitely a concentrated protein food. Cream goes through an entirely different digestive process in our system than does milk; and while it is, of course, mucus-forming to some degree, it is not in the same class of pernicious foods as milk is.

One very good thing to remember when we are overtaken by fatigue, distress, or reaction in our body is the fact that our colon is perhaps responsible for more trouble and mischief within our anatomy than all other causes and conditions put together. In our experience we have found that it is utterly impossible for a colon to develop normally and to function successfully when one lives mostly or entirely on cooked and processed foods. It is safe to assume, therefore, that it would be almost impossible to find many colons which are perfect.

This being the case, our very first step, if we are suffering from distress or reaction, would be to take a series of colonic irrigations, if possible, or, at least, a number of high enemas until the cause of the trouble had come under control. The fresh raw vegetable juices would then have better opportunity to carry on their end of the regeneration processes. The best food for the colon, we have found, is the combination of carrot and spinach juice, the formula of which is given on a later page in this book.

So many people do not have the vaguest idea of what the Colon is, what it looks like and where it is located in the body, I consider it important to reproduce here a picture of it. This picture represents one-half only of the COLON THERAPY CHART which I drew up, and which measures about 17" x 22" and is intended to be framed and hung on the wall of the office or home. (At the end of this book you will find details about it.)

Bear in mind that the quantity of juices needed by the body is predicated on their quality. Usually it will

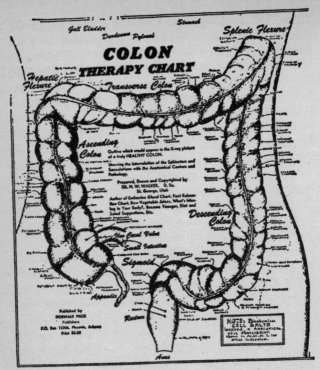

take a greater amount of juices which have been extracted by centrifugal action to get the results obtained by juices made with a Triturator and Hydraulic Press.

At all times bear this fact distinctly in mind that juices are the very finest nourishment we can get, and if we continue to take them as long as we live, the chances are that we will live a healthier life much longer than we would without them.

Carrot juice is composed of a combination of elements which nourish the entire system, helping to normalize its weight as well as its chemical balance.

It nourishes the optic system particularly, as evidenced by the many young men who applied for admission as flyers to the schools of the army and navy but were rejected at their first physical examination because of defective eyesight. A few weeks later, after drinking daily an abundance of fresh raw carrot juice, they were examined again and were accepted with the requisite of perfection of eyesight.

If this were to happen just once, it would, no doubt, be considered a phenomenon. If it were to happen only twice, it would go down into the annals of healing history as a coincidence. When it happens repeatedly, however, there is certainly sufficient reason to place doubt in the background and realize that there are more things in heaven and earth than even the most educated mind can conceive.

No less effective is the fresh raw juice of the lowly carrot in helping the treatment of ulcers and cancers. Tissues emaciated by those insidious ravages of cell starvation classified as ulcers and cancers have been nourished back to a more healthy condition by the copious use of carrot juice as the principal item of nourishment, supplementing a carefully selected and prepared raw diet.

The layman is generally awed, frightened, and puzzled at the very thought of these particular afflictions, and yet their cause and progression is really simple to understand.

When, following the European war, millions of youngsters in the desecrated regions—orphans without a home, without a roof, without a destination—roamed the country in a state of starvation, we had the picture of a national or international ulcer developing into a world-wide cancer. Allowed to spread uncontrolled, their activities would result in crimes and devastation beyond the wildest stretch of the imagination. Properly nourished and trained, they would, in a comparatively short time, become orderly and useful citizens.

So it is with the human body. Due to the deficiency of live atoms in the food people have been eating, particularly during the present and immediately preceding generations, the starved and half-starved body cells, unable to function properly and efficiently the way they are intended to, rebel and become disorganized. Not being entirely dead, these cells become dislodged from their anchorage (figuratively speaking), and float around until they find some location within the human anatomy where they can group together. With the entire body suffering more or less from live atoms starvation, there are plenty of locations in the body where protective resistance is low.

We must not conclude that ulcers and cancer result only from physical imperfections. As we have already pointed out, these ailments, and many others, may very likely stem from lifelong resentments, from stress due to states of mind such as jealousy, fear, hate, worry, frustration, and other negative intangible impediments. These are the first things to be dissolved and banished. Nevertheless we must not overlook the fact that MALnutrition and failure to maintain the system in the highest possible state of cleanliness within and without, and mentally, may definitely also be contributing factors.

Based on this premise and on the experience resulting from our researches it is our contention that the search for the cause of cancer does not lie in the field of fantastic speculation and destructive research by means of uncontrollable radium experiments, but rather in the deficiency of life in the atoms of the food we eat. On the other hand, the search for a cure would more intelligently lead us to the first principles of Godliness, namely, cleansing the body of waste matter so that the poisons therefrom should not interfere with Nature's healing processes. Simultaneously furnishing the body with an abundance of the most vital live food atoms available for the regeneration of the cells, which would enable the tissues, first, to build up resistance against further degeneration, and then, to proceed with constructive regeneration.

The sooner we realize that not a single organ in the human body works mechanically or automatically, without relation to the body as a whole, the sooner will we be able to control the functions of our system. We do not know what form of intelligence the various parts of the human organism possess nor in just what way they operate; but we do know that some inherent form of intelligence tries to protect every gland, bone, nerve, and muscle in our anatomy in spite of everything man does, usually through lack of knowledge, to destroy himself through the food he eats.

The search for the cause of any sickness or disease should lead us probably first of all to the canned food shelves of the groceries; to the flour mills; to the sugar, candy, and synthetic "soft drink" factories. Here we should investigate the products containing the dead atoms which modern civilization has attempted to develop as food and nourishment for the human body. We cannot have life and death at one and the same time, and no canned food is permitted by the government to be sold unless every vestige of life in the food in the can has been completely destroyed, for otherwise it would spoil. No cooked bread or processed cereal is eaten until it has come through the heat of the baking oven, which destroys any life element which might have been present. "Fortifying" such bread merely adds more dead atoms to it.

Analyzing the food situation from these angles, it is

obvious that whether or not we are able to live on all raw live food because of choice, environment, or circumstances, the use of an abundance and variety of fresh raw vegetable and fruit juices is fundamentally essential, bearing in mind that the vegetable juices are the builders of the body, while the fruit juices are principally the cleansers of the body. The former contain a higher relative proportion of protein elements; while the latter contain a higher relative percentage of carbohydrate elements.

It is interesting to the layman, but probably unprofitable to cancer and other similar foundations, to realize that the people who live solely on fresh raw foods supplemented with a sufficient volume and variety of fresh raw vegetable and fruit juices, do not develop cancers. On the other hand, the faith manifested by so many cancer afflicted individuals in the raw food and juices regimen seems to be a very definite indication that fresh raw carrot juice has an indisputable value in this respect.

To us this indicates a thoroughly unorthodox but, perhaps, highly efficient and much less costly line of investigation. Research along this line which has already been successfully carried on for years by those seeking and using Nature's help, may be highly disconcerting to some scientists but, undoubtedly, extremely beneficial to the one afflicted.

We have found, and we hope that the world in general will soon find, that the cleansing of the body by colon irrigations and high enemas and by eating sufficient raw food as well as drinking a sufficient volume and variety of fresh raw vegetable juices daily, will afford us little or no cause to know from further personal experience what sickness and disease feel like.

CELERY JUICE

The greatest value of raw celery lies in the fact that it contains an exceptionally high percentage of vital organic sodium. It is one of the chemical properties of sodium to maintain calcium in solution. This is particularly the case in the human system, as we will presently see.

Raw celery contains more than four times as much vital organic sodium as it does calcium. This fact makes it one of the most valuable juices for people who have used concentrated sugars and starches more or less consistently all their lives. Bread, biscuits, cakes, cereals, doughnuts, spaghetti, rice—in fact every food and food product containing flour—comes under the classification of concentrated starch. White, brown, and every kind of sugar which has been manufactured or processed, and every food product containing any of it (including candies, "soft drinks," commercial ice creams, etc.), come very definitely also under the classification of concentrated carbohydrates.

Experience has definitely taught us, however, that such foods are destructive; and their continued use results in such a nourishment-deficiency that an alarming number of ailments follow.

We have found that such concentrated carbohydrates are without question among the most destructive of our "civilized" foods. The human digestive processes were never intended by Nature to be called upon to convert these so-called foods into nourishment for the cells and tissues of the body. The result of using them is apparent in the degeneration of the human system to the point of extinction almost before adolescence has been forgotten. To consider the brief span of two or threescore years as constituting old age is nothing less than a downright insult to Nature and to our Creator. It is a shameful admission that we do not know how to live and have not taken the trouble to learn the first principles of regenerating our body. It is a confession that we eat ourselves into the grave by catering to our appetites.

In the first place, calcium is one of the most essential elements in our diet; but it must be vital ORGANIC. When any calcium-containing food is cooked or processed, as in any of the above mentioned carbohydrate foods, the calcium is automatically converted into INORGANIC atoms. As such, they are not soluble in water and they cannot furnish the nourishment which the cells in our body require for regeneration. Furthermore, enzymes, destroyed at temperatures of 130°F and over, convert the atoms into dead matter. The result is that such foods literally clog up the system resulting in such conditions as arthritis, diabetes, coronary (heart) disturbances, varicose veins, hemorrhoids, gall and kidney stones, etc.

In the second place, these deposits of inorganic calcium, being void of life, increase cumulatively when nothing is done to rid the body of them. In the presence of vital organic sodium, however, and with the assistance of other elements and processes described later in this book, they can be dislodged and maintained in solution until they have been eliminated from the system. These processes are set forth in greater detail in our discussion of Arthritis in this book.

Sodium plays a very important part in the physiological processes of the body, one of the most important being the maintenance of the fluidity of the blood and lymph in preventing their becoming too thick. The only sodium that is of any value in this respect, however, is the vital ORGANIC sodium which is derived from fresh vegetables and some fruits.

CELERY IS RICH IN SALT (SODIUM)

The "regular" Table Salt is composed of insoluble inorganic elements. Varicose veins, hardening of the arties and other ailments have been traced to the excessive use of this type of salt.

Salt is necessary in the generation and functions of digestive fluids in the system. Without salt good digestion is virtually impossible, but such salt must be entirely soluble in water.

Every cell in the body is constantly bathed in a solution of saline water, and if this is not maintained at its required level, dehydration sets in.

In the commercial production of TABLE SALT extremely high temperatures are used, running around 1500°F, to solidify the salt, with additives and adulterants to coat the salt crystals to cause the salt to pour readily under nearly all conditions.

Such salt is not completely soluble in water.

To overcome this handicap, whenever we need to use salt, we use ROCK SALT, the pure Rock Salt used, for example, in water purifiers.

Rock Salt is obtained from soil sodium rock formations and is not subjected to heat. This salt we have found to be soluble in water and its use, in moderation, of course, we have found to be compatible and satisfactory. In order to use it we grind it to the fineness we desire, in a small nut- or coffee-grinder, such as the Moulinex or any of the similar grinders sold by Health Food Stores.

Such Rock Salt is a natural catalyst which the enzymes in the body can cause to be utilized constructively.

Rock Salt will usually be found to contain the following elements:

Sodium Chloride	90 to 95%
Calcium Sulphate	.05 to 1%
Magnesium Sulphate	.05 to 1%
Magnesium Chloride	.05 to 1%

The moisture content may run from 2½ to 6% while occasionally there is a trace of "insoluble matter."

The "regular Table Salt" usually is likely to contain, in addition to the above elements in quite different proportions:

Potassium Chloride
Potassium Sulphate
Magnesium Bromide
Calcium Chloride
Sodium Sulphate
Barium Chloride
Strontium Chloride

Most of these elements tend to inhibit the dissolving of the salt in water.

During hot, dry weather, we have found it most soothing and comforting to drink a tumblerful of fresh raw celery juice in the course of the morning, and another in the course of the afternoon, between meals. This has the effect of normalizing the body temperature, with the result that we are perfectly comfortable while those around us are drenched in perspiration and sweltering in discomfort.

Sodium is one of the important elements in the elimination of carbon dioxide from the system. Deficiency of vital organic sodium results in bronchial and lung troubles, which are aggravated by the presence of extraneous matter in the lungs, such as tobacco smoke. Such deficiency is one of the concomitant causes of premature aging, particularly in women. As a matter of fact, women who smoke age about 15 years during every 5 years in which they smoke.

Nicotine is to a great extent the cause of so-called "frayed nerves." Smoking does not in any way alleviate, but rather aggravates, this condition. Any soothing experienced from the use of tobacco is mental evanescence obtained temporarily at the cost of more or less permanent degeneration of tissues, all false advertising to the contrary notwithstanding. Tobacco smoke has the effect of inhibiting the taste buds.

The combination of celery with other juices is most generally beneficial, and certain formulas have been used to help clear up deficiency, and other conditions in the body, with almost phenomenal results. When combined with other juices, the proportion of the elements in each individual juice is of course changed to correspond to the sum total of the similar elements in the other juices. Thus we get a totally different formula when juices are combined than we have in any one of the juices individually. It is the discovery of the effect of these combinations and formulas that has proved of such immeasurable benefit to ailing humanity from the cradle to the grave.

In the case of nervous afflictions resulting from the degeneration of the sheathing of the nerves, the abundant use of carrot and celery juice has helped to restore these to their normal condition and thus alleviate or remove the affliction.

Celery is very high in magnesium and iron content, a combination which is invaluable as a food for the blood cells. Many diseases of the nervous and blood system are due chiefly to the inorganic mineral elements and salts taken into the body by means of devitalized foods and sedatives.

If there is an inadequate supply of sulphur, iron, and calcium in the diet, or even if there is an abundant supply of these, but in devitalized inorganic form, then asthma, rheumatism, hemorrhoids, and other disturbances may result. Unbalanced proportions of sulphur and phosphorus in the diet may create conditions of mental irritability, neurasthenia, and even insanity. Also, many diseases hitherto ascribed to excessive uric acid in the system may really be caused by the consumption of foods too rich in phosphoric acid and deficient in sulphur.

The combination of carrot and celery juices furnishes a balance of these organic minerals in excellent combination to combat tendencies toward these diseases and help to restore the body to normalcy where these afflictions have started or taken root.

CUCUMBER JUICE

Cucumber is probably the best natural diuretic known, secreting and promoting the flow of urine. It has, however, many other valuable properties, such, for example, as the promotion of hair growth, due to its high silicon and sulphur content, particularly when mixed with carrot, lettuce, and spinach juice. It contains more than 40% potassium, 10% sodium, 7½% calcium, 20% phosphorus, and 7% chlorine.

The addition of cucumber juice to carrot juice has a very beneficial effect on rheumatic ailments which result from an excessive retention of uric acid in the system. The addition of some beet juice to this combination speeds up the general process.

The high potassium content of the cucumber makes this juice very valuable in helping conditions of high and low blood pressure. It is equally helpful in afflictions of the teeth and gums, such as in pyorrhea.

Our nails and our hair need particularly the combination of elements which fresh vital cucumber juice fur-

56

nishes, helping to prevent the splitting of the nails and falling out of the hair.

Skin eruptions of many kinds have been helped by drinking cucumber juice to which the juices of carrot and lettuce have been added. The addition of a little alfalfa juice in some cases has helped to speed up their efficiency.

DANDELION JUICE

This juice is one of our most valuable tonics. It is useful to counteract hyperacidity and to help normalize the alkalinity of the system. While exceedingly high in potassium, calcium, and sodium, it is our richest food in magnesium and iron content.

Magnesium is essential for giving firmness to the skeleton and preventing softness of the bones. A sufficient quantity of vital organic magnesium and calcium in the food during pregnancy will help prevent the loss or degeneration of teeth due to childbirth, and give firmness and strength to the bones of the child.

Vital organic magnesium in proper combination with calcium, iron, and sulphur, is essential in the formation of certain ingredients of the blood. Such magnesium has great vitalizing powers and is a constituent as a builder of body cells, particularly of the tissues of the lungs and of the nervous system.

Vital organic magnesium can be obtained only from live fresh plants and must be used fresh and raw. It must not be confused with manufactured magnesium preparations which, as inorganic minerals, interfere with the proper healthy functions of the body.

All chemical magnesium preparations, whether powdered or in so-called milk form, result in deposits of in-

57

organic waste matter in the system. While they may give the more or less immediate results claimed for them, such results are purely temporary. The aftereffects of the deposit of such inorganic matter in the body may have repercussions of a more or less devastating nature in the future. We prefer to follow in the footsteps of the sage whose principle was to be safe now rather than to be sorry later.

Vital organic magnesium, as obtained raw from vegetable juices, is a nourishing element of inestimable value to the human system.

Raw dandelion juice obtained from the leaves as well as the root, and combined with carrot and turnip leaves juice, will assist in remedying spinal and other bone ailments, as well as give strength and firmness to the teeth, thus helping to prevent pyorrhea and decay.

ENDIVE JUICE

Endive is the curly vegetable resembling lettuce, and known also as escarole and chicory. In Eastern markets the curly endive is usually known as chicory, the word endive being usually reserved for the winter-grown heads of the Witloff or Brussels Chicory, which consists of only the long, more or less straight, thick creamy-white leaves, 5 to 6 inches long by one or two inches wide, pressed closely together. This is not as rich as the green varieties of endive, as its large leaves are cut off and the roots set in cellars in sand to bleach them. Thus, this type is deficient in chlorophyll and in some of the essential minerals of which the full-grown vegetable is so rich.

Endive is closely allied to the dandelion plant, and their chemical constituents are more or less alike. Endive however, has food elements of which the optic system is constantly in need.

By the addition to endive juice of the juices of carrot, celery, and parsley, we furnish nourishment to the optic nerve and muscular system, which has brought amazing results in correcting eye defects. One or two pints daily of this combination has frequently corrected eye trouble in the course of a few months to the extent that normal vision was regained, making the use of glasses unnecessary.

One of the most outstanding cases which has come to our attention is that of a lady whose home was in West Virginia, south of Pittsburgh. Cataracts took away her eyesight completely, and for nearly three years no hope whatever was given to her that she could ever see again. She heard of miracles performed by fresh raw vegetable juices and was taken to Pittsburgh to give Juice Therapy a trial, as a very efficient plant was in operation in that city making fresh juices daily with a large Triturator and Hydraulic Press.

She followed rigidly the necessary cleansing regime, of colonic irrigations and enemas, to remove all interference by waste matter in the body; she ate only raw vegetables and fruits with no concentrated starches or sugars; she drank daily:

One pint of carrot, celery, parsley, and endive juice,
One pint of carrot juice,
One pint of carrot, celery, parsley, and spinach juice,
One pint of carrot and spinach juice.

She recovered her eyesight sufficiently in less than one year's time so that she could read newspapers and magazines with the aid of a magnifying glass!

Endive is one of the richest sources of Vitamin A among the green vegetables.

Carrot, celery, and endive juices combined, are most

helpful in asthma and hay fever, provided the cause of these conditions has been permanently removed from the diet. The cause, naturally, is usually milk and the concentrated starches and sugars.

In combination with celery and parsley, endive is very helpful in anemia and in functional heart trouble (when this is not the result of gas in the intestines), and as a blood tonic. It is also very beneficial in conditions involving the spleen.

Endive juice, in almost any combination, promotes the secretion of bile and is, therefore, very good for both liver and gall bladder disfunctions.

FENNEL (Finocchio) JUICE

There are two varieties of fennel—the common garden or sweet fennel, which is used mostly as condiment and flavoring, and Florence Fennel usually known as Finocchio and used on a very large scale by Italians and other Latin races.

The former is classified mainly as an herb and is not suitable for use in juice form except under the care of an expert on the use of herbs.

The Florence variety, however, makes an excellent juice. The plant belongs to the celery family, but its juice is much sweeter and more aromatic than celery juice. In fact, the plant is sometimes known erroneously as anise celery; but the Italian name, Finocchio (pronounced Finokkio), is that more generally used.

Fennel juice is a very valuable blood builder and is, therefore, of the utmost benefit in menstrual disorders. It has been used successfully alone or in combination with carrot and beet juice in this connection.

GARLIC JUICE

Metaphorically speaking, garlic itself is bad enough; but garlic juice by itself may cause devastating social ostracism for the one who drinks it. It is very beneficial, however, if one has the mental fortitude to overcome social handicaps, and the intestinal fortitude to endure the general discomfort which accompanies the more or less rapid housecleaning of one's system.

Garlic is rich in mustard oils and this, in conjunction with the combination of cleansing elements composing it, has a most beneficial effect on the entire system, from stimulating the appetite and the secretion of gastric juices, to the promotion of peristalsis and diuretic action.

The ethers in garlic juice are so potent and penetrating that they help to dissolve accumulations of mucus in the sinus cavities, in the bronchial tubes, and in the lungs. They help the exudation of poisons from the body through the pores of the skin, until we wonder whether the effluvium of the fragrance is any better than the dormant poisons within us.

Garlic juice has proved very effective in helping to eliminate intestinal parasites. Dysentery can be most effectively helped with this juice, and Amoebic Dysentery responds to it no less than other kinds. Parasites and germs, however, whether amoeba or any other kind, cannot live unless there is nourishment for them to thrive on. If the eliminative organs are filled with putrefactive waste matter, naturally germs will be present by the million; and if more waste matter is added cumulatively by the daily ingestion of meat, other inorganic foods, and drugs, such germs and parasites are in their element, and they propagate and multiply. This is wonderful for the germs, but disconcerting to the victim. Thus, garlic juice helps to eliminate much of this condition; but to remove the cause we find that we have to go much farther. Intestinal bathings by means of colon irrigations and high enemas have been found to be essential until the waste matter has been thoroughly cleaned out. The diet then has been so planned that the food was assimilated as completely as possible with the least liability of waste retention in the body. This has been successfully achieved with an ample supply and sufficient variety of fresh raw vegetable juices supplementing a well-balanced raw food diet.

To make garlic juice, however, almost precludes the use of the juice machine for any other juices, because once the machine has been so used, it is almost impossible to eradicate the aroma, for several days, and any juices subsequently made on that machine may be flavored with that bouquet!

HORSERADISH SAUCE

We do not use the juice of horseradish, as its ethers are quite potent and powerful enough when the horseradish is finely ground or triturated. The effect of taking one-half teaspoonful of the triturated horseradish will leave an indelible impression on the memory and a dissolving reaction on the mucus in the sinus cavities. Once this has been tried in pulp form, this impression and this reaction will no doubt solve the question of why we do not use it in juice form.

Taken in the form of freshly triturated, unpressed pulp (with the addition of lemon juice mixed with it as soon as triturated, to the consistency of a sauce) at the rate of half a teaspoonful twice a day between meals, it has effectively helped to dissolve mucus in the sinus cavities and other parts of the body without damage to the mucus membranes. It acts as a solvent and cleanser of abnormal mucus in the human system.

Used judiciously, as indicated, mixed only with lemon juice, we have found that it does not irritate the kidneys, the bladder, nor the mucus membranes of the digestive tract.

In addition to the value of the ethers in dissolving mucus, horseradish sauce is a valuable diuretic, of particular benefit in dropsical conditions.

The horseradish sauce should be prepared fresh and should not be used when it is more than one week old. It must be kept cold in a closed bottle or jar although its potency is increased if allowed to warm up to room temperature when using it. It should be moistened with plenty of lemon juice.

Horseradish sauce when taken as suggested, one-half teaspoonful in the course of the morning and one-half teaspoonful during the afternoon, daily, may at first cause a copious overflowing of tears, depending on how much mucus is packed in the sinus cavities and other parts of the system. Except for the lemon juice mixed with it, nothing else should be taken to dilute it, nor should anything be taken to drink for a few moments after eating it. This procedure has been followed for weeks or months if necessary, until the horseradish sauce could be eaten without any sensation resulting from it. It then indicated the practically complete dissolution of the mucus. For any condition of sinus mucus, this has been found a very effective natural means to help remove the CAUSE of this annoyance.

As a rule, the most satisfactory results are obtained when the mixture is in the proportion of the juice of two or three lemons to one-fourth pint of triturated horseradish to make the mixture the consistency of a thick sauce.

See the chapter covering Radish Juice.

JERUSALEM ARTICHOKE JUICE

When properly triturated and pressed, this vegetable can furnish as much as 3 pints of juice from 4 pounds of the vegetable. It is rich in alkaline mineral elements, particularly potassium, which represents more than 50% of all the rest of the mineral elements combined.

It is interesting to those who are not familiar with the derivation of the name of this vegetable to know that it is the tuber of a species of sunflower plant extensively grown in Italy and known there as the Carciofo—or Archicioffo—Girasole (Girasole meaning Sunflower); the word "Girasole" being slithered into the Anglicized "Jerusalem."

When raw, this vegetable contains the enzyme inulase and a large amount of inulin. Inulin is a substance resembling starch and is converted into levulose by the enzyme inulase. It is, therefore, a tuber which diabetics can eat with impunity. Its juice is very beneficial and palatable, whether taken alone or with carrot juice.

KALE JUICE

Kale has much the same chemical analysis as cabbage and may be used in the same manner: See Cabbage Juice.

KELP

For millions of years, rains have washed layer after layer of soil and silt down from mountains, hills and from the rest of the land. All this has gone down to the bottom of the sea, thus giving to the bed of the oceans the most fertile soil in the world.

If I were to eat flesh foods, I would choose fish, the kind of "clean fish" described in the Bible (Leviticus 11th chapter, verses 9 to 12). As fish feed on the contents of seas and rivers, their flesh naturally contains more elements—minerals and trace elements—than any other flesh.

As for vegetation, seaweed is one of our most valuable food supplements. Its roots are sometimes as much as 20,000 to 30,000 feet below the surface of the oceans, with tentacles floating to the surface where, with the help of its enzymes and the rays of the sun, it bursts forth into nodules and leaves.

The leaves are known as sea-lettuce and dulse. Dulse is an important additive to meals in Scotland, in Ireland and in many other Nations. In the United States and Canada dulse is used extensively as a dietary health food supplement in the form of dried seaweed leaves.

The seaweed with large leaves is usually dried, crushed or ground and is used in powdered or granule form as KELP.

Seaweed in any of these varieties is an excellent source of organic iodine, besides the mineral and the trace elements which are not readily obtainable in our regular vegetables.

When we consider that more than 59 of the elements in Nature are present in sea water, in solution, from the silt and soil at the bottom of the oceans, we can appreciate the value of sea food as a supplement to our nutritional programs.

The following are these 59 elements:

Actinium	Copper	Neptunium	Silicon
Aluminum	Erbium	Nitrogen	Silver
Argon	Fluorine	Osmium	Sodium
Arsenic	Gold	Oxygen	Strontium
Barium	Hydrogen	Phosphorus	Sulfur
Bismuth	Indium	Platinum	Tantalum
Boron	Iodine	Plutonium	Thallium
Bromine	Iridium	Potassium	Thorium
Calcium	Iron	Radium	Thulium
Carbon	Lanthanum	Rhenium	Tin
Caesium	Lead	Rubidium	Uranium
Cerium	Lithium	Ruthenium	Yttrium
Chlorine	Magnesium	Samarium	Zinc
Chromium	Manganese	Scandium	Zinconium
Cobalt	Mercury	Selenium	

Using Kelp and Dulse, in moderation, as food supplements, we can be fairly sure of furnishing our system with at least some of the trace elements so necessary for our wellbeing, which are not available in vegetables and fruits.

In our home we usually have a salt-shaker on our table, filled with Kelp Granules and a dish of Dulse which we use freely with our salads and with our juices.

Adding some Kelp to the Potassium Combination (carrot-celery-parsley and spinach juice), we enrich the benefit derived from this valuable mixture, and find it very beneficial for the glandular system, particularly for the thyroid gland.

Dulse and Kelp are obtainable from your Health Food Store. Do not use any of the Iodine dispensed by the drug stores on your food.

LEEK JUICE

The juice of leeks is milder than that of onions and garlic. The information on garlic juice applies to a great extent to that of leeks.

LETTUCE JUICE

Lettuce juice has many essential values to the human body. It has great quantities of iron and magnesium. Iron is the most active element in the body, and it is necessary that it be renewed more frequently than any other. The liver and spleen are the storage places for iron, where it is stored for any sudden demand that may be made upon the body, such, for example, as for the rapid formation of red blood corpuscles, in the case of a heavy loss of blood. The iron is stored in the liver for the particular purpose, among others, of furnishing mineral elements to any part of the body in an emergency, as in the case of a hemorrhage; also in the event that the food eaten does not contain the necessary quantity of this element in vital organic form.

The storage of iron in the spleen acts as an electric storage battery where the blood is recharged with the necessary electricity for its proper functions. The magnesium in lettuce has exceptional vitalizing powers, particularly in the muscular tissues, the brain, and the nerves. Vital organic salts of magnesium are cell builders, especially of the nerve system and of the tissues of the lungs. They also assist in maintaining the normal fluidity of the blood and other functions without which it would be impossible for metabolism to operate properly.

As magnesium salts can operate efficiently only if there is sufficient calcium present, the combination of these elements in the lettuce makes this food exceedingly valuable from this standpoint.

When combined with carrot juice, the properties of lettuce juice are intensified by the addition of Vitamin A in the carrot and also the valuable sodium therein which assists in maintaining the calcium in the lettuce in constant solution until utilized by the body.

Lettuce contains more than 38% potassium, 15% calcium, more than 5% iron, and about 6% magnesium.

Lettuce also contains more than 9% phosphorus, which is one of the principal constituents of the brain, and an ample supply of sulphur, which is one of the component parts of the hemoglobin of the blood, acting therein as an oxidizing agent. Many nervous afflictions are due chiefly to these two elements, sulphur and phosphorous, taken in inorganic form, as in cereals and meat.

Together with silicon, of which lettuce contains more than 8%, sulphur and phosphorus are essential in the proper maintenance and development of the skin, of the sinews, and of the hair. It is due more to the excessive quantity of these elements in their inorganic form in a diet of cereals and devitalized food, that hair roots do not obtain their proper nourishment; hence one of the reasons for loss of hair.

Drinking daily an abundance of a juice composed of carrot, lettuce, and spinach, will furnish food to the nerves and roots of the hair; and by this means the growth of hair can be stimulated. Hair tonics in this respect are of little or no value except that they furnish massaging for the scalp. They cannot feed the hair but merely stimulate the action of the nerves and blood vessels and so assist the proper food in reaching the hair roots through the blood stream.

Another efficient juice combination to help the

growth of hair and restore it to its natural color is carrot, lettuce, green pepper, and fresh alfalfa juice. (See preceding chapter on alfalfa juice.)

When making juice from lettuce for definite therapeutic purposes, it is best to use the leaves that are of the darker shade of green, omitting those which are inside the head of lettuce and have remained white, as the former are much richer in chlorophyll and other vital important elements than the latter.

The juice of lettuce leaves has been a great boon and relief to those suffering from tuberculosis and from gastric disturbances. It is also a valuable diuretic.

Because of its richness in iron and other valuable vital elements, lettuce juice has been given to infants, with carrot juice, with highly satisfactory results, whether they were breast- or bottle-fed.

COS or ROMAINE LETTUCE JUICE

Although a member of the lettuce family, Romaine Lettuce has an entirely different chemical composition from that of Head lettuce. It originated in the Island of Cos, in the Greek Archipelago, and in Great Britain it is known as "Cos Lettuce."

The juice of Romaine Lettuce, with the addition of a small amount of kelp (seaweed), has been found to contain properties conducive to helping the activity of the Adrenal Cortex in its function of secreting its hormone, Adrenalin, to keep the body in balance.

Its particular value lies in its rich sodium content which is 60% higher than its potassium content. This makes it one of the most beneficial juices where this particular relative proportion is essential, as for example, in Addison's Disease, in which the adrenal glands are affected, requiring the maximum amount of vital organic sodium with a relatively low percentage of potassium to compensate for Adrenal Cortex hormone deficiency.

In the treatment of this disease we have seen some remarkable results when an ample supply of fresh raw juices was used daily in which this chemical composition more or less prevailed. The diet was held rigidly to the elimination of all concentrated starches and sugars, all meat of every kind, and all vegetables containing an excess of potassium over sodium. This narrowed the choice of vegetables and their juices to:

Beets, celery, Romaine lettuce, spinach, and Swiss chard. Also included in the diet were fresh pomegranate, strawberries, tomatoes, and figs, honey, almonds, and beechnuts.

Fresh raw carrot juice was added to all or any of the above juices with much benefit. In some extreme cases, some fresh raw goat's milk with carrot juice was found helpful.

On this basis, with a regular cleansing program by means of colonic irrigations and high enemas, excellent results were obtained.

MUSTARD GREENS JUICE

Mustard greens are valuable in salads. The high content of mustard oil, when the greens are made into juice, may be irritating to the alimentary tract and to the kidneys. Mustard greens contain a high percentage of oxalic acid; they should therefore never be eaten when cooked. Read the chapter on Oxalic Acid.

Although the juice of mustard greens, by themselves, may cause some discomfort, nevertheless, a small quantity in combination with carrot, spinach and turnip juice

70

has been used with much benefit to help dissolve hemorrhoids.

As in watercress, the sulphur and phosphorus percentage is very high in the mustard greens; and their effect on the system is almost identical to that of watercress. See Watercress.

ONION JUICE

Somewhat milder than garlic, with a less pungent aroma, onions and their juices do, without question, build us up physically to a remarkable degree, while at one and the same time they tear us down socially.

What we have said about garlic applies quite fully to the onion and its juice, bearing in mind that what may be termed the repellent atmosphere of the garlic and its juice is somewhat subdued in the case of the onion.

PAPAYA JUICE

While papaya is definitely a fruit and not a vegetable, it is pertinent to refer to it here because of its remarkable therapeutic qualities.

Until comparatively recently this fruit was practically unknown in the North, as it is strictly a tropical fruit.

Not unlike a melon or a squash in shape, it matures in many sizes from less than one pound to as much as 20 and more pounds each.

Its particular qualification for our attention is its juice, when the green fruit is triturated and pressed, containing a principle known as papain, which has much the same digestive effect as pepsin in our digestive processes; it also contains fibrin, a principle rarely found except in the body of man and animals. It is readily digestible in gastric and pancreatic juices and is especially

71

valuable in the coagulation or clotting of blood, either superficial or internal.

The green, unripe papaya has much more active papain enzymes than the ripe, this activity being somewhat dissipated in the ripening processes. The juice of the green papaya has helped correct intestinal disorders, including ulcerous and more serious conditions, in an incredibly short time.

We have frequently seen the crushed pulp, including the skin, of the green papaya applied as a poultice to serious lacerations, and the following day hardly more than the scar was apparent. We had a finger seriously crushed in a machine, and the application of a similar poultice left the finger usable within two or three days.

As a juice, both the green and the ripe papaya are unsurpassed as a remedy to help nearly every affliction of the body. Truly, Nature has given us in this fruit the most comprehensive means as first aid in both internal and external ills.

PARSLEY JUICE

Parsley is an herb.

Raw parsley juice is one of the most potent of the juices. It should never be taken alone in quantities of more than one or two ounces at a time unless mixed with a sufficient quantity of carrot or other raw vegetable juices such as celery, lettuce, or spinach, and even then, in not too great a proportion in relation to the volume of other juices.

Raw parsley juice has properties which are essential to oxygen metabolism in maintaining the normal action of the adrenal and thyroid glands. The elements in parsley are proportioned in such a manner that they help to maintain the blood vessels, particularly the capillaries and arterioles, in a healthy condition. It is an excellent food for the genito-urinary tract, being of great assistance in conditions of calculi in the kidneys and bladder, albuminuria, nephritis, and other kidney troubles. It has been used effectively in dropsy.

It is also efficient in every ailment connected with the eyes and optic nerve system. Weak eyes, ulceration of the cornea, cataracts, conjunctivitis, ophthalmia in all of its stages, or laziness of the pupil, have been effectively treated by drinking raw parsley juice mixed with carrot juice, and with carrot, celery, and endive juices.

Never drink too great a quantity of raw parsley juice by itself, as its high concentration may result in a disarrangement of the nervous system. Taken with other juices properly mixed, it is extremely beneficial.

Strictly speaking, parsley belongs to the herbs classification; hence its highly concentrated effect. It is used effectively to help promote menstrual discharge, particularly in conjunction with beet juice or with beet, carrot, and cucumber juices. Cramps as a result of menstrual irregularities have been relieved and frequently corrected entirely by the regular use of these juices when concentrated starch and sugar foods have been omitted from the diet.

RAW POTASSIUM BROTH

There are many vegetables rich in potassium, the most outstanding of which are carrot, celery, parsley, and spinach. To obtain the full value of this potassium element, it should be taken as a drink in its raw, undiluted state so that the body may absorb and assimilate it completely in its natural form.

The organic minerals and salts in this combination of raw potassium "broth" embrace practically the entire

73

range of those required by the body. Its effect in reducing excessive acidity in the stomach has been truly remarkable. There is probably no food more complete in every respect than this for the human organism.

When the sick are unable to assimilate other food, it has been found that raw potassium broth has usually furnished the nourishment to bring the patient back to normal. In the case of convalescents, raw potassium broth is invaluable, and it is astonishing that all hospitals and sanitoria have not adopted this food as a regular part of their daily diet.

Some people do not find Potassium as palatable as the straight carrot juice or some of the other juice combinations. We must bear in mind, however, that when the body is starved for the live atoms of food so essential for the regeneration of the cells and tissues of the body, the time has passed when the matter of taste has any bearing whatever on the choice of the juices we need.

As we have already previously stated, no drug in the entire Pharmacopoeia will supply the body with the live organic food atoms, vitamins, and hormones essential for the regeneration of the wear and tear that results in sickness and disease. Such food is most quickly obtained by the body when we drink fresh raw vegetable juices.

As the atoms composing the cells and tissues of our anatomy are mineral and chemical elements, and the glands, organs, and in fact, every part of the system represent combinations of such atoms in certain definite patterns, so we are able to determine that certain combinations of chemical and mineral live elements in our food, and particularly in our juices, can nourish corresponding parts of our body.

PARSNIP JUICE

This juice has a very low calcium content and much less sodium, but is very rich in potassium, phosphorus, sulphur, silicon, and chlorine. Because of the low calcium-sodium content, the all-round food value of this vegetable is not as great as that of some of the other tubers; but the therapeutic value of the juice of its leaves and root place it high on the list of beneficial juices.

The rich silicon-sulphur content is most helpful in correcting the condition of brittle nails. The phosphorus-chlorine elements are of particular benefit to the lungs and the bronchial system, thus making this juice an excellent food for tubercular and pneumonia victims, and those afflicted with emphysema.

The high potassium content is of such excellent value to the brain that this juice has been effectively used in many mental disorders.

WARNING: The foregoing all applies only to the cultivated parsnips. The wild variety must not be used in juices because it contains some poisonous ingredients.

PEPPER JUICE (GREEN)

This juice has an abundance of silicon which is greatly needed by the nails and the hair. The tear-ducts and sebaceous glands also benefit greatly from the use of this juice.

In combination with carrot juice, in the proportion of one-quarter to one-half of green pepper juice to the rest of carrot juice, it is an excellent aid in clearing up skin blemishes, particularly if colonic irrigations and enemas are taken with sufficient regularity to remove waste matter from the colon while the cleansing processes within the body are progressing.

Those bothered with gas or wind in the alimentary canal, and those suffering from colic, flatulence, or griping, have found much relief from drinking at least one pint daily of this juice combination in conjunction with one pint of carrot and spinach juice. Of course, these juices need not be taken at one time. In fact, drinking them at the rate of one tumblerful at a time with intervals of one, two or three hours in between, have given better results. We prefer to drink them before and between meals.

POTATO JUICE

The raw potato contains easily digestible natural sugars which, upon cooking, are converted into starch. Potatoes should be omitted from the diet of those suffering from venereal diseases and those afflicted with aphrodisiac tendencies. The combination of cooked meat and potatoes intensifies the solanine poison of the potato (an alkaloid poison more particularly prevalent in potatoes too green in color), which has an affinity for the nerves controlling the sexual organs; this, together with presence of uric acid crystals resulting from the ingestion of meat, may cause excessive irritation of these organs.

The juice of raw potatoes, however, has proved very beneficial in clearing up skin blemishes. This cleansing is due to the high content of potassium, sulphur, phosphorus, and chlorine in the potato. These elements, however, are only of value when the potato is raw, in which state they are composed of live organic atoms.

When the potato is cooked, these are converted into inorganic atoms and, as such, they are of little or no value for constructive purposes.

Fresh, raw, organically grown potatoes are very palatable to eat, many people do like them and they are unquestionably a good food.

Raw potato juice has proved to be a healthy cleanser of the system and to be very beneficial, particularly in combination with carrot juice.

The juice of raw potatoes, combined with that of carrot and celery, is a boon to those suffering from gastric, nerve, and muscle disturbances, such as gout and sciatica. In such cases, one pint of this combination in addition to one pint of carrot, beet, and cucumber juice, daily, has often given complete relief from these discomforts in a surprisingly short time, provided that meat, fowl, and fish were eliminated completely from the diet.

Some emphysema victims have been helped and found relief in using a combination of carrot, parsley and raw potato juices.

SWEET POTATO, botanically, is not in any way related to the ordinary or "Irish" potato. It contains one-third more carbohydrates in the form of natural sugars than the Irish potato, three times as much calcium, twice as much sodium, more than twice as much silicon, and more than four times as much chlorine.

The juice of sweet potatoes has, therefore, more general beneficial value than that of the Irish potato. Care must be exercised, however, in choosing them, as they are more readily spoiled by bruises and decayed spots, which quickly affect the whole tuber, than the Irish potatoes, which will stand more rough and careless handling with impunity.

RADISH JUICE

This juice is extracted from the leaves and the roots, but should never be taken alone, as it is too strong in its reaction if taken by itself. In conjunction with carrot juice, the combined elements help to restore the tone of the mucus membranes in the bidy. It is used most effectively about one hour after taking horseradish as described in the chapter covering that subject. It has had the effect of soothing and healing the membranes and cleansing the body of the mucus which the horseradish sauce has dissolved. It has at the same time helped to regenerate and restored the mucus membranes to their normal state.

Nearly one-third of the natural content of radishes is potassium, while, of the remaining two-thirds, more than one-third is sodium. The iron and magnesium content are both high, and it is from these that the healing and soothing qualities to the mucous membranes have been found.

It is usually unnecessary in most cases to undergo surgical operations for the removal of the mucus which causes sinus troubles. While such operations remove some of the mucus, the aftereffects eventually may be devastating. The horseradish sauce on the other hand, as described, has repeatedly given lasting benefits. Mucus is the result of drinking too much milk and eating concentrated starches, bread, and cereals in excess.

RHUBARB JUICE

Rhubarb is probably responsible for more kidney trouble among children than any other single factor. Few if any other plants have such a high concentration of oxalic acid as rhubarb. When cooked, this acid is converted into an inorganic chemical which, when eaten, deposits vast amounts of oxalic acid crystals in the body.

Innumerable cases of rheumatism and rheumatic fever could be traced to the ingestion of cooked rhubarb. No example could be more vivid than this to prove the fallacy of eating some food or food product because of certain individual particular merit, without regard to the disastrous effect of other elements it may contain. Because of its supposedly laxative properties, rhubarb is used extensively for children as well as by adults. Because the laxative results are more or less immediately apparent, no further thought is given to the other end product—the oxalic acid crystals deposited in the body. As these deposits do not cause immediate irritation and their effect is insidious and slow in manifesting itself, the consequences are rarely if ever attributed to the proper cause—the eating of rhubarb.

The subject of oxalic acid is so very important that we have covered it fairly extensively in a separate chapter under that heading, which see.

Some benefit can be derived from fresh raw rhubarb juice, however, provided that it is used sparingly, and only in combination with other juices such as carrot, celery, or fruit, and their combinations. In this manner it can help stimulate the peristaltic action of the intestines. Never sweeten rhubarb with sugar, use honey.

SAUERKRAUT JUICE

Sauerkraut is a preparation of pickled cabbage, finely cut and fermented in brine composed of a great deal of salt. This pickling and fermentation is exceedingly injurious to the mucus membranes of the ailmentary canal and affects adversely the texture of the skin, tending to coarsen it. Its stimulating effect on the digestive organs is very detrimental because of the presence of so much of the inorganic salt solution.

SORREL JUICE

The juice of the broad-leafed French Sorrel is excellent in helping the sluggish and prolapsed intestines to re-establish their normal functions, when such necessary steps as colonic irrigations and enemas are taken to eliminate the accumulation of waste matter collected therein.

This vegetable is rich in potassium oxalate, which is valuable for the human system only in its vital organic raw state. It should never be eaten when cooked.

It contains a particularly large percentage of iron and magnesium, which the blood needs constantly, and vast amounts of the cleansing elements phosphorus, sulphur, and silicon which are used by every part of the system from head to foot.

The combination of these rich elements makes this juice most valuable for nourishing all the glands in the body.

SPINACH JUICE

Spinach is the most vital food for the entire digestive tract, both the alimentary section of the body (the stomach, duodenum, and small intestines) and for the large intestine or colon, and it has been so recognized from time immemorial.

In raw spinach, Nature has furnished man with the finest organic material for the cleansing, reconstruction, and regeneration of the intestinal tract. Raw spinach juice properly prepared, taken at the rate of about one pint daily, has often corrected the most aggravated case of constipation within a few days or weeks.

The use of purgatives for the cleansing of the intestinal tract is, unfortunately, practiced without an understanding of exactly what takes place. Every manufactured chemical or inorganic purgative or laxative acts as an irritant, stimulating the muscles of the intestines to expel IT. With the expulsion of this irritant, other matter lodged therein may also be expelled. It is obvious, and in practice it is proved to be a fact, that the habit of taking laxatives necessitates stronger and stronger irritants. The result is not a cure for constipation, but a chronic condition of inactivity of the local tissues, muscles, and nerves.

Cathartics are merely irritants and while they remove some of the waste matter, they cannot possible cause other than progressive degeneration of the intestines.

Furthermore, such methods of cleansing the intestinal tract are solely temporary in their effect and furnish no material for the regeneration or building up of the weakened or degenerated tissues, muscles, and nerves. (Read the chapter "TO DETOXICATE" which goes into this matter in detail.)

The use of saline purges has a different effect. A saline solution passed through the intestinal tract draws from the lymph stream large quantities of lymph. One 8-ounce glass of Pluto water, for example, may eject one whole gallon of waste matter and toxic fluid from the lymph stream through the colon, which will usually be found to be excessively acid and loaded with poison from body waste. Unless this acid, toxic, or poisoned lymph so expelled is replaced by an organic alkaline solution such as natural raw fruit juices, the final result is an inevitable water deficiency in the body. Also, if such replacement or realkalinization is not taken care of, then in the natural course of events during the activities of the body, poisons remaining in the intestinal tracts will, by reabsorption, find their way into the lymph stream, again aggravating the condition that the individual was trying to correct.

Raw spinach juice, on the other hand, very effectively cleanses and helps to heal not only the lower bowels but the entire intestinal tract.

The spinach works by natural means to repair the most essential damage first; it is not always apparent to the individual where in his body the work of regeneration is progressing. Results may not be noticeable sometimes for as long as six weeks or two months after daily consumption of this juice.

It has been found essential at all times, however, that the bowels be cleared never less than once in every twenty-four hours, although the normal, healthy condition calls for two or three movements a day. The colon can be washed out with colonic irrigations or enemas, or both if necessary, every day. This has been found most effective in the long run.

Another valuable feature of raw spinach juice is its effect on the teeth and gums in helping to prevent pyorrhea. This disease is a mild form of scurvy and results from a deficiency in the body of the elements found particularly in the combination of carrot and spinach juices. Bleeding gums and a fibroid degeneration of the pulp of the teeth has become a common defect due to the habitual use of devitalized cereals, refined sugar, and other deficiency foods. It is due to a Vitamin-C deficiency.

A permanent aid for this affliction has been found in the use of natural raw foods and, more particularly, in drinking an ample quantity of carrot and spinach juice.

Other derangements of the body such as duodenal

and other ulcers, pernicious anemia, convulsions, degeneration of various nerves, deficiency in adrenal secretions and those of the thyroid, neuritis, arthritis, abscesses and boils, pains in the region of the gonads, swelling of limbs, tendency to hemorrhage, loss of vigor, rheumatic and other pains, impaired functions of the heart, low and high blood pressure, eye troubles, and headaches, including those of a migraine character, are due primarily to the cumulative volume of waste matter in the lower intestine; also, to the dificiency of the elements contained in raw carrot and spinach. The quickest and most effective way in which the body can obtain and assimilate these elements is by drinking daily at least one pint of the fresh raw vegetable juices.

Spinach, lettuce, and watercress are, together with carrots and green peppers, among the vegetables containing the best supply of Vitamins C and E. The lack of a sufficient quantity of Vitamin E in the system is a contributing factor responsible for miscarriages, as also for impotence and sterility in both sexes. Many forms of paralysis are due to a lack of Vitamin E which is responsible for general lack of well-being and impaired metabolism.

When spinach is the subject matter of discussion, one generally associates it with its effectiveness as a laxative. The underlying cause for this effectiveness is the high oxalic acid content in this vegetable. This is such an important element involved in the activities of our intestines that it is worthy of very special attention, and we have given a whole chapter to the subject of oxalic acid, which see.

Spinach should never be eaten when cooked unless we are particularly anxious to accumulate oxalic acid crystals in our kidneys with the consequent pain and kidney trouble. When spinach is cooked or canned, the oxalic acid atoms become inorganic as a result of excessive heat and may form oxalic acid crystals in the kidneys.

OXALIC ACID

One of the mysteries of the human anatomy is that function which is known as peristaltic motion. This motion, or action, takes place in the alimentary canal, in the circulating and generative tubes, and in the eliminative channels, in successive wavelike motions, forcing whatever matter is present therein, onward on its course. It is a series of contracting and relaxing of the nerves and muscles successively—a function which takes place involuntarily so far as our own voluntary controlling powers are concerned, and apparently is entirely automatic.

The efficiency of this peristaltic action, however, is very naturally dependent on the tone and healthy and vigorous condition of the nerves and muscles of these channels.

Organic oxalic acid is one of the important elements needed to maintain the tone of and to stimulate peristalsis. It is perfectly obvious, of course, that any motion of the body which takes place by the "involuntary" action of its organs is predicated on there being life in the cells and tissues of such organs. Life is active, magnetic; whereas there is no action in death nor in dead matter, and this applies definitely to cells and tissues of our anatomy.

If the important organs comprising the alimentary and eliminative departments of our system, or any parts of them, are moribund or dead, the efficiency of their function is impaired, to say the least. This condition can result only from a lack or deficiency of live atoms in the food nourishing the cells and tissues concerned. Live food means that food which contains live organic atoms and enzymes found only in our raw foods.

We have already, in previous chapters, covered this important question of organic versus inorganic atoms in our food. It is very vital to stress this matter in regard to oxalic acid. When the food is raw, whether whole or in the form of juice, every atom in such food is vital OR-GANIC and is replete with enzymes. Therefore, the oxalic acid in our raw vegetables and their juices is organic, and as such is not only beneficial but essential for the physiological functions of the body.

The oxalic acid in cooked and processed foods, however, is definitely dead, or INORGANIC, and as such is both pernicious and destructive. Oxalic acid readily combines with calcium. If these are both organic, the result is a beneficial constructive combination, as the former helps the digestive assimilation of the latter, at the same time stimulating the peristaltic functions in the body.

When the oxalic acid has become INORGANIC by cooking or processing the foods that contain it, then this acid forms an interlocking compound with the calcium even combining with the calcium in other foods eaten during the same meal, destroying the nourishing value of both. This results in such a serious deficiency of calcium that it has been known to cause decomposition of the bones. This is the reason I never eat cooked or canned spinach.

As to the oxalic acid itself, when converted into an inorganic acid by cooking or processing the food, it often results in causing inorganic oxalic acid crystals to form in the kidneys.

It is worthy of notice that the minerals in our foods— iron, for example—frequently cannot be assimilated

85

and used completely if they have become inorganic through cooking, and often prevent the utilizing of other elements through chemical and other action. Thus, the iron in fresh raw spinach juice may be utilized 100%, but only one-fifth of that, or less, would be usable in cooked spinach.

It is well to bear in mind, therefore, that, as the organic oxalic acid is so vital to our well-being, the fresh raw juice of the vegetables containing it should be used daily to supplement the eating of these raw vegetables included in our daily salads.

The most abundant supply of the organic oxalic acid is found in fresh raw spinach (both the common variety and the New Zealand spinach), Swiss chard, beet greens, turnip and mustard greens, kale and collards, and the broad-leafed French sorrel.

TOMATO JUICE

This is probably one of the most widely used juices—out of cans. Fresh, raw tomato juice is most beneficial and has an alkaline reaction if digested when no starches or sugars are present in concentrated form; but if these are present and eaten or drunk during the same meal, then the reaction is definitely acid.

Tomatoes have a fairly high citric and malic acid content, and some oxalic acid. These acids are all needed and beneficial in the processes of metabolism, provided that they are vital organic. When tomatoes are cooked or canned, these acids become inorganic and, as such, they are detrimental to the system, although their injurious effect is insidious and may not manifest itself immediately. Some instances of kidney and bladder stones are the result of taking cooked or canned tomato or its juice, particularly with starches and sugars.

Fresh raw tomato juice is rich in sodium, calcium, potassium, and magnesium.

There are innumerable varieties of tomatoes, all of which, if used fresh and raw, make excellent and beneficial juices.

STRING BEAN JUICE

This juice is of particular benefit to diabetics. Diabetes is a dietary disease resulting from the excessive consumption of concentrated starches and sugars, and is aggravated by the consumption of meat.

It is definitely conceded that the hypodermic injection of Insulin does not furnish a cure for this disease. Diabetes is not a hereditary disease. It may, however, be caused by the hereditary habit of the excessive use of concentrated carbohydrates. The feeding of inorganic, cooked flour and grain products and pasteurized or boiled cow's milk to infants is the contributing factor in the development of diabetes in children and adolescents primarily, and in adults eventually.

Insulin is a substance that the pancreatic gland secretes to enable the body to properly utilize natural sugars (not the manufactured sugars) as fuel for energy to carry on its activities. As we have already previously pointed out, the body can only use, constructively, the natural vital organic sugars which fresh raw vegetables and fruits furnish in abundance. It cannot use starch nor manufactured sugars as such, but must reconvert them into "primary" sugars. Starch is an inorganic product and the sugars which are converted from it in the body are, of course, also inorganic. Inorganic elements have no enzyme life or vitality. The pancreas therefore works overtime in this reconversion process, only to receive lifeless atoms in return, which have no regenerative or constructive quality whatsoever. This results in what is known as diabetes.

The fact that excessive adipose tissue accumulates in diabetics is the result of the false inorganic Insulin stimulus, which not only does not burn up the waste matter, but actually helps it to accumulate.

It has been found that string beans and Brussels sprouts when made into juice, contain elements which furnish the ingredients for the natural insulin for the pancreatic functions of the digestive organism.

In cases of diabetes, the entire elimination of all concentrated starches and sugars of every nature whatsoever, and the drinking of a combination of the juices of carrot, lettuce, string beans, and Brussels sprouts at the rate of about two pints daily, besides one pint daily of carrot and spinach juice, gave results which were satisfactory and beneficial. Of course, colonic irrigations and enemas were used regularly and liberally.

TURNIP JUICE

No vegetable contains as high a percentage of calcium as the juice of turnip leaves, the calcium being more than one-half of all the other minerals and salts combined.

It is therefore a most excellent food for growing children and for anyone having softening of the bones in any shape or form, including the teeth. By combining turnip leaves juice with carrot and dandelion juice, we obtain one of the most effective means of helping the hardening of the teeth as well as the entire bone structure of the body. The very high magnesium content of the dandelion together with calcium in the turnip leaves and the elements in the carrot combine to give the bone structure firmness and strength.

The potassium content is also very high in turnip leaves, which results in this being a strong alkalinizer, particularly when combined with celery and carrot juices. It is therefore excellent to reduce hyperacidity. Turnip leaves also contain much sodium and iron.

Calcium deficiency, strange as it may sound to the uninformed, results very frequently from drinking pasteurized cow's milk. Of course, the constant use of concentrated flour, grain, and sugar products also results in calcium deficiency because, although these products have an exceedingly high calcium content, this type of calcium is just as inorganic as that used in making cement.*

The cells and tissues of the body cannot use this type of inorganic calcium atoms for constructive purposes, with the result that the blood stream must move them out of the way so they will not interfere with its operations and activity.

Just as we brush things aside that interfere with our own freedom of action, so the blood sweeps many of these inorganic atoms into the terminal ends of blood vessels. As the most convenient of these are located in the rectum, they receive a gradual accumulation of this debris until they enlarge enough to be uncomfortable, when their name is changed to Hemorrhoids.

As most people include an excessive amount of devitalized, inorganic food in their daily meals, it is only natural to find that probably one-half of them have hemorrhoids, and know it, while the remainder may have them and do not know it.

We have not known a single case of hemorrhoids among the many adults of all ages who have been lifelong abstainers from these inorganic foods. On the

*Read more on this subject in the Book DIET & SALADS, by N. W. Walker, D.Sc.

other hand, we have seen an unending procession of victims victimized by attempts to cure this natural affliction by means of injections, electric coagulation, and surgery with no permanent results, because the manifestation was attacked instead of the cause.

We had one very typical case come to our attention. It was a prominent lawyer whose protruding hemorrhoids were painful, distressing, and embarrassing to the nth degree because he could not walk many blocks without having to stop in the first inconspicuous place to propel them back into place.

This gentleman had been drinking a variety of juices daily for many months without telling anyone of his main trouble. He modified his diet slightly, still eating his meat and potatoes, bread, doughnuts, and other injurious foods, with little or no apparent effect on his affliction.

One day he wagered the owner of the juice bar of which he had become a regular customer, that no juice could help hemorrhoids; whereupon, he was asked to drink two pints daily of a combination of carrot, spinach, turnip, and watercress juices, and follow rigidly a raw vegetable and fruit diet, and watch results.

In less than one month this lawyer came to the juice bar, jubilant, after having been carefully examined by his physician who declared that there was no indication whatever of his erstwhile hemorrhoids.

This is not one isolated instance. This combination of juices has helped innumerable sufferers when they adhered rigidly to natural foods and natural methods.

WATERCRESS JUICE

This juice is exceedingly rich in sulphur, which represents more than one-third of all the other mineral elements and salts combined in the watercress. Nearly 45% of the elements in watercress are acid forming, including sulphur, phosphorus, and chlorine. As it is a very powerful intestinal cleanser, it should never be taken alone, but should always be used with other juices, mixing it, for example, with carrot or celery.

Of the alkaline elements, potassium predominates, being slightly more than 20%; while calcium is about 18%, sodium, 8%; magnesium, 5%; and iron about one-fourth of one per cent.

A combination of carrot and spinach juice with some lettuce, turnip leaves, and watercress juice, contains the components essential for the normal regeneration of the blood and particularly for increasing oxygen transmission in the blood stream. For anemia, low blood pressure, and underweight, this forms an excellent food combination.

A combination of carrot, spinach, turnip leaves, and watercress juice has the property of helping to dissolve the coagulated blood fibrin in hemorrhoids, or piles, and many kinds of tumors. Two pints of this combination taken daily, when all flour and sugar products, and preferably also meat, have been eliminated from the diet, have been found to dissolve these conditions in from one to six months in a perfectly natural manner, provided that there has been no surgical interference, in which event it may take longer. Read the chapter covering Turnip Juice, in which the question of hemorrhoids has been gone into more fully.

Watercress Juice is a valuable adjunct to carrot, parsley and potato juices, as a combination, to help emphysema victims. The predominance of phosphorus and chlorine has thereby proved to be beneficial.

OH! SO YOU HAVE A COLD—HAVE YOU?

Is your breathing congested? Are you sneezing? Do you have a general "let-down" feeling?

For many, many years investigators have been, and still are, attempting to find, to isolate and to identify some evanescent, evasive "germ" to blame for the common cold.

Sometime during the middle 1920's science made the headlines with the "discovery" of a "germ" which was definitely responsible for the common cold, but that it was too small and elusive to be caught or even to be visible by means of the most powerful microscopes then available. Yet, they "discovered" such a "germ" ! ! ?

In the march of progress in the field of enlarging the image of matter, electronic microscopes have made such vast strides that what is virtually invisible can be magnified many thousands, even hundreds of thousands, of times. Scientists are still playing with the thought that "the germ" can be caught, but to my knowledge and as a result of all the research and investigations which I have been able to make, no such "germ" has yet been seen, caught or harnessed.

During the past 23 years—actually since 1946—according to word I have from England, some "Scientists," under the $150,000 a year patronage of the British Government's "Medical Research Council," have been hunting—and, you know, the British are notorious for their hunting!—for a COLD BUG, a GERM or VIRUS as the culprit, which could be blamed for or accused of being responsible for the starting or the generation of the COMMON COLD.

So far, from every available report they have not yet, after 23 years, been able to find, catch, harness nor "develop" one. Surely they have been able to identify about

100 different germs, virus or bacteria, but not one of these was able to start a cold. Every one of these was feeding on the mucus of Common Colds, the very purpose for which they were created, namely to dissolve, break up, decompose and so dispose of the mucus that manifests the Common Cold.

As I understand it, these British "Scientists" have some kind of a research hospital where they not only invite people to come there and stay for 10 days or so, free of charge, all meals and everything else provided, but patients are paid something like five shillings a day to come there and submit themselves to the Scientists' attempts to find a germ or virus that will GIVE them a cold. It has become quite a fad for some 30 people at a time to go there once or twice a year for a very inexpensive vacation, with pay.

I understand that so far only a handful of people during the past few years did develop a cold, but the germ or virus that was supposed to create it has never yet been discovered.

No, indeed, there is not a germ in existence which can cause one to have a cold. The electrical analogy in reference to a cold is worth remembering. The electric system in your home is equipped with fuses. Right? What happens when the electric circuit is overheated because you have overloaded the line with too many lights and appliances? Does a "germ" notify you that a fuse will blow out or that the overheating of the wires may burn down your home? No, indeed. If the fuse fails to blow out, the overloaded and overheated wires will start a fire.

Think this over when you "catch a cold."

The waste matter in the system, if not eliminated, builds up fermentation and heat in the body in the natural course of events. When such fermentation has reached a sufficiently toxic state, Nature becomes worried about our neglect to keep the body clean, within, and gives us a warning in the form of mucus elimination which has been labeled "a cold." It is just as simple as that, and we have seen it demonstrated over and over and over again, that if the warning is ignored and disregarded, more serious conditions develop, conditions which are so well known that a list of them covers a medical encyclopedia.

Never curse a cold which has caught up with you. Rather be thankful for the timely warning, and do something about it. No drug was ever known to cure a cold without the development of eventual afflictions of a more serious nature, rarely attributed to such drugs.

To put it briefly, a cold is the result of the secretion of too much accumulated waste, and insufficient and improper elimination. The Colon is the recipient of all this corruption. Toxins spread throughout the body generating unhealthy mucus in the sinus cavities. Excessive waste matter is the contributing factor in the generation of mucus. The result—A COLD.

An intelligent individual will give due consideration to these facts, and as a matter of course will do what innumerable other people have done at the first signs of a cold, namely, take high enemas and colon irrigations to remove the cause. Fruit juices and fasting for a day or two—using nothing but water and fruit juices—have been very effective during such cleansing procedures.

A regimen of raw foods and juices has been found to be the best means to prevent the accumulation of waste and mucus when the body, and the colon in particular, has been kept consistently clean.

YOUR ENDOCRINE GLANDS

The human body could not function were it not for the ENDOCRINE GLAND system. The glands in our body are the activating mechanisms responsible for, and involved in, every function and procedure taking place within our system.

There are glands of internal secretion and glands of external secretion. These glands all manufacture in micro-microscopic quantities a substance known as HORMONES.

Hormones are a product generated and elaborated in the glands and discharged into the blood or lymph, in most cases, while in some instances their action is somewhat like making an electrical contact in one place, to start, stop, or to modify an action in a separate and perhaps remote place.

Endocrine means that the manufacture of hormones takes place within the gland, with no duct for its discharge from it. The discharge takes place by osmotic transmission from within the gland through its covering, and is collected by the blood or the lymph from outside the gland.

Glands of external secretion are those with a duct or ducts leading directly from the generating plant in the gland, out of the gland into the blood or the lymph or into its environment. The Tonsils and the Appendix are external secretion glands, the former injecting its product into the throat, while the Appendix injects its product into the colon.

The volume of hormone secreted at any one time is so infinitesimal, so infinitely small, that in order to obtain one-quarter of an ounce of the Pineal Gland Hormone extract, for example, it would be necessary to collect hormones from more than 20,000,000 individual glands!

Like every other part of the human body, glands must have constant nourishment in order to be able to operate efficiently. Such nourishment should be of the very finest quality, because of the important, the intricate and the delicate work which the glands are called upon to perform.

I have made and drawn a Chart of the Endocrine Gland System, showing the human form, and radiating from it are explained and indicated the various Endocrine Glands and their relation to one another. It indicates the nature of their function and of their disfunction, it reviews what stimulates them and what inhibits them, it lists the elements of which they are composed and shows what fresh raw vegetable juices we have found to be of help and benefit for their well-being. This Chart measures about 17" by 22" and is intended to be framed for hanging on the wall of your study, of your office or of your home.

(Endocrine Gland Chart can be obtained from Aurora Book Companions Co., Terminal Box 5852, Denver, Colorado, 80217, or your Health Food Store can get it for you.)

The extensive ramifications of the hormone chain is nothing short of stupendous, and even a superficial study of this Chart is enough to make us appreciate our Eternal Creator for furnishing our insignificant body with such a marvel of ingenuity.

The least we can do to help our wonderful glandular system to function at its highest state of efficiency is to keep our body thoroughly cleansed of waste and corrupt matter, to nourish the body with the best natural raw foods and juices available, and learn to completely control our mind and our emotions.

With due and careful attention to this program, we should acquire the energy we need to live a full, happy, useful, joyous and intelligent life.

VINEGAR

All references in my previous publications to the injurious effects of VINEGAR applied definitely ONLY to the white distilled vinegar and to wine vinegar, in which the destructive element is the predominance of acetic acid.

Pure apple cider vinegar, on the other hand, made from whole apples, and not diluted, contains the constructice MALIC ACID, an ingredient needed in the digestive processes.

There are three kinds of Vinegar which are generally used. In this country, Apple Cider and the white distilled Vinegar. There is also Wine Vinegar which is a commonly used condiment in Latin countries, and which, like the White Distilled Vinegar, contains ACETIC ACID.

White Distilled Vinegar is injurious to the system. It rapidly destroys red blood corpuscles, resulting in anemia. It also interferes with the digestive processes, retarding them and preventing the proper assimilation of food. Such Vinegar ($C_2H_4O_2$) is the product of the fermentation by acidity of alcoholic fluids such as fermented wine and malt liquors; these are known as Wine Vinegar and Malt Vinegar respectively. The White Distilled Vinegar with a high acetic acid content is widely used in this Country.

Vinegar made from apples is known as APPLE CIDER VINEGAR. It contains MALIC ACID ($C_4H_6O_5$) which is a natural organic constituent of apples and is an element involved in the digestive processes.

Vinegar made by the process of fermentation of wine contains on an average of from 3% to 9% Acetic Acid, and usually some Tartaric Acid in addition. Acetic Acid in Vinegar has been known to be a contributing factor in causing hardening of the liver (cirrhosis of the liver), duodenal and other intestinal ulcers, etc.

APPLE CIDER VINEGAR, on the other hand, contains MALIC ACID, a constructive acid which combines with alkaline elements and minerals in the body to produce energy or to be stored in the system as glycogen, for future use. It has proved to be of immeasurable value when used judiciously by humans and for animals.

Space does not permit the publishing, here, of beneficial results obtained. For example, in how it helps in the coagulation of blood, in establishing a normal menstrual flow, and contributes to healthy blood vessels, veins and arteries, and in building red blood.

One of the great virtues of APPLE CIDER VINEGAR is its extraordinary potassium content, an element so necessary for building and storing body reserves and to help the system to achieve harmony and calm. This potassium readily associates with some of the most important elements in the body, such as calcium, sodium, iron, magnesium, chlorine, silicon, etc.

It is important, when choosing Apple Cider Vinegar, to consider its source, in order to be sure that it is made from whole apples, and not the kind that is cheaply made just from apple cores and peelings.

Used judiciously, Apple Cider Vinegar is an indispensable item for the kitchen cupboard. Its antiseptic qualities are almost beyond belief. Many victims of skin blemishes, even of the contagious type, have been helped by the application of Apple Cider Vinegar directly on the skin.

In Scotland it used to be, and perhaps it still is, a common practice to shrink varicose and "bulging" veins by the application of Apple Cider Vinegar on the skin to the whole length of the veins, morning and night, for a month or so, and at the same time drinking daily two or three glasses of water with two teaspoons of Apple Cider Vinegar in each glass. And it worked!

Your LIFE is manifested in the condition of your blood which is generated in the marrow of your bones, activated through your spleen and circulated through your blood vessels. It is a natural, systematic process that causes the blood stream to be completely re-created every period of 28 days, and unless the balance is maintained between the creation of new blood cells while the old blood cells complete their cycle, health cannot be maintained and one's efficiency is impaired.

In the maintenance of balance in body competence no single class of nourishment has proved as effective as the fresh raw vegetable and fruit juices. Likewise, no individual means to help obtain the quick re-establishment of such balance has proved to be as efficacious as pure apple cider vinegar.

Excessive bleeding in menstrual cycles, bleeding hemorrhoids, nose bleeding, cuts, etc., have been wonderfully helped by drinking two teaspoons of apple cider vinegar in a glass of water, daily, and two or three times a day if necessary.

When there is a deficiency of hydrochloric acid in the digestive system which results in the failure of the system to properly digest proteins, giving rise to high blood pressure, apple cider vinegar has been used, one to three teaspoons in a glass of water during the meal, with a consequent perceptible lowering of the blood pressure.

ON THE SUBJECT OF MILK

Whenever MILK, other than Mother's Milk, is needed, RAW GOATS' MILK is the most logical and beneficial Milk for humans of all ages to drink.

Milk should NEVER be heated at temperatures above 118° F, because at 130° F the Enzymes are destroyed. We should NEVER use pasteurized milk for the same reason. It is best, when possible, to use it as soon as practical after the goat has been milked, before the milk is refrigerated. However, kept cold in a sealed bottle in the refrigerator it will keep and be perfectly good for a day or two.

It cannot be too strongly emphasized that for infants there is no better milk than mother's milk. The next best is fresh RAW Goats' milk.

Recently my attention was directed to the little 22-months' old daughter of a good friend of ours. The mother nursed the child for one year, and up to that time, and for many months after, the child never had so much as a "running nose" nor one upset day, physically nor in her disposition, until one day she was given pasteurized goat's milk. It happened that the child's father kept two goats. One day these "dried up." He tried to get some RAW Goats' milk from a goat dairyman, but the dairyman told him he could not legally sell the milk to him RAW. It had to be pasteurized. Under the dairyman's pressure and arguments my friend bought a quart of pasteurized Goats' milk and fed it to his child.

Within two days after drinking the pasteurized milk the child's nose started "running" and she became irritable. Her father immediately went out and bought two "fresh" Goats, giving the child the RAW Goats' milk.

In two days the child's disturbances disappeared!

This child drinks regularly RAW Goats' milk and fresh raw carrot juice.

This is by no means a rare occurrence. On the contrary.

Raw Goats' milk is one of the cleanest foods we can use, whereas cow's milk is rarely clean. Cow's milk has been proved to be very mucus forming, whereas goat's milk is not.

In the Book of Proverbs, chapter 27 and verse 27, we read:

"And thou shalt have goats' milk enough for thy food, for the food of thy household, and for the maintenance of thy maidens."

The reason Goats' milk is not generally used today is purely an economic one. A cow yields a much larger volume of milk than does the goat. The vast City and Urban populations are the deterrent to the general use of goats' milk. A great many more farm hands would be needed, for example, to milk 500 goats to get the yield which 100 cows would give.

To keep goats we need a shed only about 10' by 12' to shelter five goats, and these five goats need LESS feed than one cow would require.

Of course, the ideal situation is for one or two families to acquire 4 or 5 acres of tillable land, with plenty of water available, with about one or more acres of this in trees. Keep two or three milk goats, a small flock of good poultry which would feed in the fields, a vegetable and fruit organic garden with a flower garden and two or three beehives to yield 60 or 75 lbs. of honey a year or more.

On such a set-up one can be independent, particularly if funds are available to own the place free and clear. One would need little more than one's Social Security to live comfortably, and have a long healthy, happy and useful life.

Such a dream CAN come true. Do not let an inferiority complex deter you: others have done it—you can. Remember the old proverb: Aim at the sky and you'll hit higher than a tree.

Reverting back to the milk problem. Remember that the goat is probably the cleanest animal we have. Its eliminative organs are close to perfect. Hence her disposition is friendly—almost loving. Her milk has a vastly higher vibration than the milk of the cow, and is of certainly higher vibration than that of the mother who smokes, who drinks "soft drinks" and whose temperament may conservatively be classed as "touchy" if she has a brood of children who rule the home and their parents.

Besides being the cleanest of animals, goats are virtually free from tuberculosis, brucellosis and others of the ailments which afflict the cow.

The quality of goats' milk is far superior to that of the cow, being naturally homogeneous, having more non-protein nitrogen, better quality of proteins, with much higher amounts of niacin and thiamine than almost any other food or food product.

Goats' milk has been known to be most beneficial and efficient in cases of diarrhea in small children. This is due to its extremely high niacin content.

Thiamine is one of the most important of the B-complex vitamins, involved in all of life's vital processes, from birth to the grave. Goats' milk abounds in thiamine.

Let me emphasize again that it is best not to heat Goats' milk to more than 118° F. Goats' milk overheated or boiled, including pasteurization, is better poured down the drain than fed to children. If pasteurized goats' milk is fed to the kids of the goat, they will likely be dead within six months.

NATURAL CHILDBIRTH

Baby Eric slipped into the World with a squawk! !

This is the detailed account of what Diane Vallaster Folton did during the period of her pregnancy and how Baby Eric has been thriving on RAW FOODS. No "Baby Formulas." Read it, and in the future: GO THOU AND DO LIKEWISE!

Here are Diane's own words:

There it was, June 1966 and I was pregnant! I was due to have my first baby at the age of 33. What an astounding and sobering thought! One month of school still to go, thirty grade one students to keep busily occupied, as well as attend to endless end-of-the-year forms, left me feeling limp.

Suddenly the vegetable salads I had been enjoying so much, felt like sawdust in my mouth—my diet formed a completely new pattern. Roughly, it went as follows:

1, 2 and 3 months pregnant: Nothing appealed to me but grapefruit and freshly cracked hazelnuts (filberts) eaten three times a day.

4, 5 and 6 months: Though grapefruit was still a staple, I found myself back to enjoying a wide variety of fruits. By this time we were in September and the wild blackberries were at their tangy best. We also managed to find delicious plums, prunes, pears and apples all grown without chemicals. We had read that raspberry leaf tea was good for pregnancy, so early in September we visited our neighbors' raspberry field and picked

103

bags of leaves which we dried on trays and then stored. From September until March first, I consumed at least a pint of this tea daily. It was difficult to find good carrots, but we managed to obtain enough for a pint of the precious juice a day. Because I was exhausted after a busy school year, I felt I needed a few supplements to boost me along, so I took daily:

6 kelp tablets,

6 natural calcium tablets,

100 I. U. of Vitamin E,

2 teaspoons of cod liver oil, because we are just not out in the sun this time of year in British Columbia, Canada.

And natural Vitamin C in varying quantities.

If ever there was any retention of water in my system, I immediately hunted for a fresh pineapple, if none was available I found that the unsweetened pineapple juice worked also.

I was feeling so wonderful that I never saw a doctor until the sixth month. Friends were becoming so alarmed that I finally consented to see one. The doctor could not get over the strong heartbeat the babe had, that I had no weight gain, and that I had no toxicity. He believed in natural childbirth so he was pleased with my simple natural diet.

I hiked miles every day. We had two puppies so I always had an excuse to be out. I took a course in prenatal exercises for natural childbirth and did them daily as well as my housework.

Then, at last, March first, Eric slipped into the World with a squawk and a head of thick long curly black hair. The hair was so remarkable because most babies born now have little or none. His glowing color was the talk of the doctors and nurses—no milky white skin for him!

To the amazement of everyone, I was able to breast

104

feed Eric, and though the milk was slow in coming, I persevered, and soon there was an ample supply of rich creamy milk, although I had always been told that such milk is usually blue and watery.

The hospital diet was rather dead after the live foods that I had been eating, but I ordered every live or living food that was offered on the menu. The nurses were constantly worried that my protein intake was inadequate, so I was bombarded with huge glasses of pasteurized milk every three hours. These I fed to the sink and replaced them with water. My husband and my sister brought a quart of fresh carrot juice to me each day, plus bags of freshly shelled hazelnuts to supplement my meager diet. The tray of sundried fruits that I was presented with was pronounced "dangerous" as—they said —it would give the baby diarrhea. I could not see how it could hurt baby or me, as I had eaten them for ten years and baby had done a beautiful job of growing on it for nine months already.

How wonderful it was to return home to an abundance of all the foods I was used to. I could no longer resist the tray of dried fruits and, as we expected, there were no ill effects!

With all the raw food I was eating (at least 60% of which was fruit) I was horrified, after Eric was born, that he went day after day without a bowel movement. Finally, on the fifth day home, he produced a completely normal small stool—no constipation! No diarrhea!

Where had the stool been so long? We were mystified, but this was to be the pattern. How often I wondered if I should give him enemas. The mystery continued until, by chance, we found an old baby book on breast feeding, stating that the food was sometimes so completely utilized that it was not unusual for a wee babe to go up to seven days without a bowel movement.

This pattern continued as long as he had no solid foods. At six months of age he sipped a little fresh carrot juice, but it was not until he was nine months old that he had any solid food. Very ripe banana and a wee bit of avocado, both pressed through a fine strainer, made up his first solid meal.

Thereafter there was no waiting five days for his bowel movement. In the space of a few hours after eating, he produced a stool full of tiny black threads! I was horrified! Now (I thought) he must have worms! The public health nurse was due in our area that day. I tearfully met her at the door and presented the diaper for her inspection. She immediately wondered what he had eaten, and when I told her just a bit of banana, she laughed and said: "Well, there are your worms: banana cellulose!" To this day I find it hard to believe that a soft banana is so full of cellulose!

Eric had only these two foods—banana and avocado —plus a little carrot juice until he was more than one year old. Slowly, then we added the pulp of strained soaked raw prunes, dates, and apricots, usually accompanied by avocado, to his diet. Soon he was having blended fresh fruits as they came in season.

Eric was the chooser of his food, we soon learned. Sometimes he had only apples for days at a time. Then he would switch to avocado, and so it went. He loved, and still loves, to chew on dried dulse leaves.

The only milk he received was breast milk for two and a half years. Now he drinks carrot juice, nut milk, and we hope to start him soon on raw goat milk.

He has never had a stuffy head, no mucus, no puffyness, no distended stomach and no swollen glands.

Most of my friends were busy feeding their babies pablum, and from bottles. The pablum supposedly to keep them sleeping all night. Since their babies were unable to digest the starch, it was a never ending round of colds, flu, pneumonia, diaper rash and allergies. Thankfully we have escaped all of these by following the simple but rigid laws of Nature.

One thing that bothered me about nursing was the fact that I required more sleep and did not have my usual extra bounding energy—but I had a happy contented baby instead. I also noticed that my stomach did not go flat as I had expected, but after Eric stopped nursing it resumed its normal proportions.

Now it is May, 1970,—Eric is three years of age. His diet consists of raw and dried fruits, fresh raw vegetables and their juices, nuts, seeds and honey. He is well balanced mentally, well developed physically, and full of energy and curiosity.

My many thanks to Dr. Walker's Program.

DO JUICES HELP BONES TO HEAL? HERE'S THE ANSWER!

This is the letter I received from Adelle Vallaster, a Home Economics Teacher, in Kamloops, B.C., Canada:

Finally, after years of planning, Mom and Dad left for Europe, while we attempted to look after their Health Shop. The postmen went on strike at this time, a further complication to our situation. All communication was at a standstill until that fateful telegram arrived ten days before Mom and Dad were due home. We were instructed to send extra money, to have "Bob" meet the plane with his car, and for us to start planting boxes of wheat grass.

Something was radically wrong! There was no way of knowing what—until they arrived home. Ten anxious days: we learned that a motorcycle had bumped into Mom as she was crossing a street in Austria having all but severed her leg. By some miracle she was treated by one of the leading bone specialists in the area, and he succeeded in placing the terribly fragmented bones in position so that they had a chance to knit.

Mom's one idea was to get home as fast as she could to her raw juices and foods, for she knew of so many cases where healing had been so wonderfully helped in this way.

Two weeks after the accident, they were due to return to Canada. The doctor in Austria thought that they were mad to even think of going. He felt that for one thing Mom would not be able to bear the pain of being shifted around so much. Dad, on the other hand, felt so strongly that he must get her home. Finally the doctor gave his consent. Mom managed the trip very well due to her wonderful health from having been on the Walker Program for ten years.

As soon as she arrived home we started the flow of Juices—4 oz. of wheat grass juice three times a day, carrot juice and an untold number of cups of comfrey tea —both root and leaf. She also had extra help from a natural Vitamin C, natural calcium, and Vitamin E. We had an abundance of organically grown peaches, pears, grapes and apples to supplement our supermarket salads that fall and winter. Each afternoon she had a mixture of sunflower seeds and sesame seeds finely ground and mixed with a little honey, plus yet another cup of comfrey tea.

The doctor, here, wanted to take her into the hospital immediately, as gangrene had set into the wound. After much persuasion he finally agreed to leave her home so long as the condition did not worsen, and that we take her to the hospital regularly to change dressings. This was a problem, but a solution was quickly found.

How we would love to have been able to put comfrey and wheat grass poultices on the wound, but with only a tiny slit on the casting for air and instrument dressing, this was impossible.

The condition held its own for about three weeks; then there was a noticeable healing from the inside out. This was an unheard of occurrence since no wonder drugs had been used. Only live juices and foods were supplying the elements needed for healing. The condition continued to improve steadily and hospital visits became less frequent.

Six months later when the cast came off, the nurses were astounded to find that there was no odor as is usual when a cast has been on for so long. When X-rays were checked, the small bone had knit but not the large one, so another long cast was put on. The doctor was quite certain that it could not heal and that a lot of grafting, both of bone and flesh, would have to be done because the break was so jagged, with the healing surface so large, and because so much bone marrow had been lost.

The doctor used to tell the nurses, jokingly, that this was the lady who expected God and the greens to heal her, but when the cast was removed, two months later, with both the bones completely knit, the doctor was the most amazed witness!

Now, twenty-one months after the accident, flesh is steadily filling in the scar. At first, there was literally just skin over bone. Now, Mom walks without the aid of a cane, goes to the Health Shop each day, and does her own shopping. Thanks to God and the Walker Program.

PARENTS AND YOUR CHILDREN
(ALSO FOR MANY ADULTS!)

Illiteracy is a handicap not limited to the adolescent nor to the underprivileged adult!

I take the following appropriate extract from the booklet FACTS ABOUT PHONICS by Mrs. Marie A. LeDoux, producer of the PHONICS principles known as PLAY'N TALK:

"The reading dilemma was forcibly brought to my attention during the early "fifties" when as President of 26 privately owned Corporations, I personally observed Junior Executives as well as Secretaries unable to comprehend what they read. These college credentialed employees also frequently misspelt words in their reports."

Success in life hinges to a very great degree on the person's ability to READ. You, for one, would not appreciate this very book if you were not able to read; and perhaps, to you, it is inconceivable that there could be people who cannot READ!

One of the greatest problems of the present generation is the fact that more than a million youngsters a year leave High School before they graduate. Their handicap is that they have not learned to READ. SUCH dropouts are facing a jobless future.

Millions upon millions of men and women between the ages of 18 and 50 are in the "Poverty Class" because they cannot read, write and spell properly, if at all.

In my own school days, reading and writing were tedious, prolonged and protracted hours and days of constant effort to LEARN these essential arts. The results justified every effort made under the strict direction and guidance of teachers who were dedicated EXPERTS on these subjects. The result? I read, write and understand what I see in print.

Today, unfortunately, there are far too many teachers whose reading, writing and spelling leave much to be desired. Under such tutelage how can we expect all students to attain any degree of perfection in this matter?

PHONICS is the science of sound as it applies to each letter or group of letters. According to the Saturday Review (January 1962) ". . . to the child learning to read, many words are unfamiliar and a knowledge of phonics is essential. It should be included in every reading program and should be commenced early . . ."

PHONICS is like a magic key that serves to UNLOCK unfamiliar words and open the door to the wonderful world of reading. Learning to read "by PHONICS" is merely converting the letters into their respective sounds. After learning isolated sounds, short vowel families are structured into one-syllable words, which are immediately used in sentences.

Good spellers, who have mastered the phonics principles, develop an auditory concept whereby they convert the sounds used in words back into their respective letters.

Recorded lessons on LONG-PLAY discs, coupled with illustrated texts, make it possible for the student, whether at home or in the classroom to SEE while listening to the sound of the voice instructing in detail how to pronounce and how to classify each word.

By this means, children from Kindergarten age to adults in business have learned to read, spell and write successfully in a matter of weeks or months, instead of the two or three years required by the memorizing methods so lamentably prevalent in present day teaching.

111

Without the use of PHONICS, love of reading is discouraged, the vocabulary is limited and spelling becomes a problem.

Here are a few examples, taken at random, of the benefits derived from the use of PHONICS.

Los Angeles, California: A "Chef," 55 years old, grown up in Texas Oil Fields, with no formal elementary education, earning $35 a day in Texas, could only earn $15 a day in California because he was unable to READ! He obtained the basic course in PHONICS and only five weeks later announced: ". . . I am now back to $35 a day as a "chef," because I can READ!"

NOTE: For the Adult who has never used phonics, the teacher on the record makes possible an easy "do-it-yourself" listening program for studying in private and at the adult's convenience.

Office personnel, Junior Executives, Secretaries, File-clerks, etc., who have never learned phonics may increase their earning power by perfecting this skill. Besides, a mastery of the sounds of one's native tongue as they relate to language skills, facilitates learning of foreign languages.

Only 10 minutes daily for about 8 or 10 weeks, with the teacher's voice on the records, makes this simple and easy. Results can be obtained with amazing speed. Imagine being able to read, pronounce and understand, not only English, but foreign languages as well! From Los Angeles: The mother of a young child writes: "My daughter has enjoyed the first records very much and is ready for the second series. I might add that I have gotten a lot from the records, also, as I have never had PHONICS."

From Harbor City, California: Mrs. J. T. writes: "The first and most important result of your records is that it teaches children to study in an orderly day-by-day system, which has been completely lacking in the school my three boys attend. They have finally mastered the sounds of the consonants and most of the vowel sounds in the books. I showed one of the teachers the records and books and she was very enthusiastic about them. There are many children in the 4th and 5th grades who are UNABLE to read."

Missionary reports from South Africa: "Now the children can read their Bible and come to know God."

Australian lady writes: "Reading has taken a new meaning—anything that's fun is no longer work."

Mrs. James H. N. . . ., Pittsburgh, Penna., writes: "Last December we invested in your records to assist our nine-year-old with his reading . . . A week ago (June 1969) the final report was received along with his rating . . . taken a few weeks ago. His teacher has called us to express her pleasure at his progress and his new found confidence. Jim now knows he can read; new words no longer present stumbling blocks but challenge his knowledge. While his reading grade was C, other subjects where reading is essential, he received A's and B's. The Stanford places him above-average in 5 subjects and average in 3, compared to 7 average and 1 above-average last year. His teacher feels he has matured a great deal but the phonics knowledge has created 'an achiever.'

"The amazing part of this is that Jim has not completed the second series of records. Jim has asked me to help him finish the records, which I expect to do this week.

"Mr. N. . . . and I cannot find words adequate enough to express our appreciation for your phonics system. We will continue to sing our praises and urge others with children having reading problems to contact your Foundation."

From Teacher in Carpenter School, Downey, California: "After using it two weeks with a second grade group who had just been promoted from the first grade, I saw improvement in word recognition. The top and middle groups were interpreting meaning of words with ease. They began to read silently without audible vocalization—a remarkable accomplishment. At the end of the 4-week session they were reading units of story material of more advanced level, and could relate a whole story with accuracy of sequence."

Ventura, California: Mrs. W. E. writes: "Thought you might like to hear the wonderful progress of one of our sons since using the records. In three weeks his teacher commented on a terrific change in his "sounding-out" his words—he is a second grader. She has seen such a change in his reading habits—he is being promoted to the high reading group—this was accomplished in three short weeks with these records. We should have found you sooner. Again thanks!"

Mrs. C. A., Deer Park, Long Island, N.Y., writes: "I couldn't begin to tell you how satisfied I am with the results. My 6-year-old has improved immensely and now has a much better understanding of sounds and words. My 5-year-old who just entered Kindergarten already reads. It is fantastic. I have told all my friends about these records. It is unfortunate that they are not advertised more widely. They could be of such help to so many children and parents. Bless you."

From Landsdowne, Penna., Mrs. R. C. K. writes: "My 5-year-old has completed series No. 1 and reads with self confidence that I never thought could exist in a child her age. I look forward to each day knowing that she will be happier as a result of learning to read properly and effectively."

From Dallas, Texas, Mrs. Evelyn B. writes: "We

have completed the series I and II and feel that our 10-year-old has the helpful fundamental rules to assist her in sounding out new words. The long and short sounds of vowels has always frustrated her in sounding out new words. This area is covered so well in the records."

From Los Angeles, California, Mrs. N. S. writes: "After one month my 5½-year-old son has quickly gone through the five records. He sounds out words on billboards and reads from the newspaper. Just lately, he sounded out the word 'conversations' doing it syllable by syllable."

I consider these testimonials a remarkable demonstration of the efficacy of Mrs. LeDoux' principle and teachings.

As a contribution to the crusade against illiteracy, the NON-PROFIT=PLAY 'N TALK READING PROGRAM makes available, FREE, the following:

PLAY 'N TALK PHONICS CHART (9" x 14") useful for teaching initial sounds or to check phonics ability.

HIGHLIGHTS IN PHONICS: 20-minute "Long-Play" record. Provides sampling of the basic course, plus data regarding the value of PHONICS in all aspects of learning.

FACTS ABOUT PHONICS: A 40-page book showing the pro's and con's about PHONICS. Documentation regarding PLAY 'N TALK, plus a complete catalog.

All these items listed above can be obtained direct from:

PLAY 'N TALK International Headquarters, P.O. Box 18804,

Oklahoma City, Oklahoma 73118, U.S.A.

by sending to them your request by printing your name,

address and ZIP code number, plus only 25¢ for handd-
dling.

* * *

As further pertinent information, I would like to add
that fresh raw carrot juice, drinking one pint a day, and,
in addition, drinking one pint a day of fresh potassium
juice (Formula No. 2 in list of Formulas on a subsequent page) daily, has shown remarkable scholastic at-
tainments achieved by students.

It is my opinion that fresh raw vegetable juices together with PHONICS, could make an unbeatable combination. Try it.

THINGS TO BEAR IN MIND

1. *Be patient:*
   In the reconstruction or regeneration of the body by
natural means, it is very important to bear in mind that
natural foods taken in the form of vegetable juices may
start a regular housecleaning process throughout the entire system. This may be, and sometimes is, accompanied by a period of pains or aches in the regions of the
body where this housecleaning is taking place. It may
even at times make one feel as if he were actually sick.
We should not for one moment feel that the juices are
making us ill, if these are fresh and are taken the same
day that they are made. On the contrary, we should realize that the cleansing and healing process is well on its
way, and the sooner such discomforts are felt after taking plenty of juices, the better, because we will be over
them just so much quicker. The more juices we drink,
the faster is the recovery. When in doubt, it is best to
consult a doctor whose practice includes an understanding of Juice Therapy. Unless a doctor has used
juices consistently, he cannot reasonably be expected to

116

know much about them and their effect. To deprecate or to denounce fresh raw vegetable juices, and particularly carrot juice, as harmful in any way, manner or form, is to admit a reprehensible lack of knowledge.

We must not expect that a lifetime accumulation of toxins can be squeezed out of our body in a miraculous way, overnight. It takes time.

2. *Be tolerant and compassionate!*

It has been claimed by writers of comic news that carrot juice will turn the skin yellow. It is ignorance of the functions of the body that would make anyone believe such nonsense. It is just as absurd to expect the color pigment of the carrot to come through the skin as to expect the red of the beet or the green of the spinach to come through. Whenever, after drinking juices, yellow or brown appears through the skin, it is an indication that the liver is eliminating stale bile and other waste matter in greater quantities than the eliminative organs can handle so that some of the elimination takes place through the pores of the skin, which is perfectly normal. If the body is toxic, such may also be the case. When we continue to drink vegetable juices, however, the discoloration eventually disappears.

There are times when, through overwork or excessive exercising and through lack of sufficient sleep, even though we feel that our body is in pretty good condition, such discoloration may appear. After rest, however, this discoloration generally vanishes, sooner or later.

In any case, once our body has been regenerated by the continuous regular use of natural raw foods and fresh raw vegetable and fruit juices, and it has been cleared of waste and obstructions, we have such a superabundance of health, energy, and vitality that the criticism of uninformed critics fails to affect us.

117

3. *Sanitation:*

The proper cleaning and sterilizing of the machinery in which juices are made and of all the utensils and of the premises is of paramount importance. Raw vegetable juices are extremely perishable, and every care possible must be taken to make them in a sanitary manner.

When using a home machine, just as much as in a factory, juices should never be made in a machine which was not first rinsed with cold water, then cleaned with boiling water immediately after it was used the last time unless it is first thoroughly sterilized with boiling water and then cooled with cold water before using it.

Sometimes juices will spoil in spite of the most meticulous care in sterilizing the equipment. This may be due to the fact that one or more of the vegetables was spoiled, affecting the entire batch. It is, therefore, of extreme importance to clean the vegetables thoroughly and to remove any part that is wilted, mushy, or spoiled.

TO DETOXICATE:

Supreme cleanliness is the first step toward a healthy body. Any accumulation or retention of morbid matter, or waste of any kind, within us, will retard our progress towards recovery.

The natural eliminative channels are the lungs, the pores of the skin, the kidneys, and the bowels.

Perspiration is the action of the sweat glands in throwing off toxins which would be injurious to us if retained in the body. The kidneys excrete the end products of food and body metabolism from the liver. The bowels eliminate not only the food waste but also waste matter known as body waste, in the form of used-up cells and tissues, the result of our physical and mental activities, which if not eliminated cause protein putrefaction resulting in toxemia or acidosis.

The retention of such body waste has a much more insidious effect on our health than is generally suspected, and its elimination is one of the first steps toward perceptible progress.

One efficient method to effect such elimination quickly, particularly in the case of adults, has been found useful through the following procedure, namely:

(NOTE: Do not use this detoxication in the case of appendicitis or if there is a tendency toward it.)

First thing in the morning, upon arising, we drink one 8-ounce tumbler full of saline solution, such for example as Pluto Water, or mix one tablespoonful of Glauber Salts (Sodium Sulphate) in an 8-ounce tumbler of water (warm or cold). The purpose of this saline solution is not primarily to empty the bowels, which however, it will do anyway, but rather to draw into the intestines from every part of the body such toxic matter or body waste as may be present, and to eliminate it through the bowels.

If such a saline solution cannot be taken or obtained, then we use Seidlitz powders, taking one powder dissolved in water, immediately upon arising, and one every 15 minutes thereafter until altogether six powders have been taken.

This saline solution acts on the toxic lymph and body waste just like a magnet acts to attract unto itself nails and metal filings. This body waste is thus drawn into the intestines and out of the body in a series of copious eliminations from the bowel, which may amount altogether to about one gallon or more.

If nothing were done to replace in the body something in volume equal to the quantity of matter so eliminated, then the body would naturally be dehydrated to that extent. Therefore we replace the toxic or acid material so removed by drinking two quarts of citrus fruit juices, freshly extracted, diluting them with two quarts of water for quicker absorption into the body. This should have an alkaline reaction on our system. These citrus juices are prepared fresh and in the following proportions, namely:

4 large or 6 medium size grapefruit,

2 large or 3 medium size lemons, and

enough oranges to complete a total mixture of two quarts.

Add to this 2 quarts of water.

We drink one 8-ounce tumblerful, beginning half an hour after having taken the saline solution or the sixth Seidlitz powder, as the case may be. We follow this with a tumblerful of these diluted juices every twenty or thirty minutes thereafter until the whole two quarts of juices diluted with two quarts of water are finished.

We do not eat anything all day, although if very hungry toward evening, we may take some oranges or grapefruit or their juices, or some celery juice.

Before going to bed at night, we take a high enema in the knee chest position, using two quarts of water slightly cooler then tepid, into which the juice of one or two lemons has been added.*

We use preferably a 30-inch colon tube, and lubricate it with HR or KY jelly (water soluble vegetable lubricants) instead of mineral jelly such as vaseline.

If you have difficulty obtaining such a colon tube, your Pharmacist can no doubt get one for you from The FAULTLESS RUBBER COMPANY, address: Ashland, Ohio, 44805.

The purpose of this enema is to remove from the

---

*Read illustrated chapter on enemas in Dr. Walker's book "BECOME YOUNGER," published by the Norwalk Press.

folds of the colon and bowels any waste matter which may have remained lodged there and which might otherwise be absorbed into the system during sleep.

We repeat this detoxication for three consecutive days. Thus, approximately three gallons of toxic lymph will have been eliminated from the body and will have been replaced by three gallons of alkaline juices. This has resulted in speeding up the re-alkalinizing of the system.

On the fourth and subsequent days, we begin taking vegetable juices and vegetables and fruit, all raw.

We need not be unduly alarmed if we feel somewhat weak during or after this detoxication. Nature uses our energies for a housecleaning within us, and we soon regain greater energy and vitality as a result of a cleaner and healthier body.

(NOTE: If there is the slightest tendency toward appendicitis, we would not use this method but take only high enemas (or colon irrigations if possible), two to three or more daily for one week, or longer if necessary.)

RAW VEGETABLE AND FRUIT JUICES AND THEIR THERAPEUTIC USE IN SPECIFIC AILMENTS

For Children and Adolescents Use In Reasonable Proportions

To facilitate the description of the juices which have been used most efficiently to help the following ailments, their various combinations have been listed; the numbers indicated in the case of each ailment will cor-

(*DIET & SALAD SUGGESTIOS, by N. W. Walker, D.Sc., published by Norwalk Press.)

respond to the formula number in the list of juice combinations on pages 125 through 131.

For adults, at least one pint daily of one or more of the formula combinations indicated have been taken over a period of several weeks to obtain perceptible results.

The juices for each ailment are given in the order of their greatest efficacy according to our experience, those which we found essential being indicated in bold type, the others having also proved effective. When possible, at least one pint of each combination whose formula number is indicated in bold type was taken daily. For example: In the case of ARTHRITIS, at least one pint of Formula No. 22 (grapefruit); also, one pint of No. 61 (carrot and spinach combined); also, at least one pint of No. 6 (straight celery juice); and at least one pint of No. 37 (carrot and celery combined) was taken. This means a total of four pints daily, which usually gave perceptible results within a reasonable time. The addition of one pint of No. 30 (carrot, beet, and cucumber combined) was also found very beneficial. These juices were taken throughout the day at intervals of one or two hours between each combination.

We must remember that by combining one or more different kinds of juices we change the chemical combination of each individual one so that the effect of the combination as a whole will be entirely different from that of each juice if taken separately and individually; and it is by the knowledge of these proper combinations that we have been able to get results that seem unbelievable to those who lack this experience.

In the selection of the juices and their combinations which have proved most beneficial for specific ailments or conditions, it is necessary to study the underlying cause and attack it in order to remove the manifestation.

In the case of arthritis, for example, for which we have given the various formulas that have proved most beneficial, we find that it is usually due to long retained RESENTMENTS, and to the result of the accumulation of inorganic calcium deposits in the cartilage of the joints.

As the afflicted cartilage has a magnetic attraction for inorganic calcium atoms, the blood deposits them there instead of in some other part of the anatomy, such as in the case of hemorrhoids. In arthritis they solidify the cartilage and ligaments, while in hemorrhoids they form a coagulated blood fibrin. In either case, the eating of foods containing these inorganic calcium atoms does not create even the slightest suspicion of what eventually may take place.

Once an arthritic deposit has taken root, however, it becomes progressively menacing until actual bone distortion may take place. The enlargement of the joints is usually the first manifestation after the occasional shots of sharp pain at shorter or longer intervals make themselves felt. Once the incrustations of this calcium have established themselves, their headway becomes a matter of routine and their deposit becomes cumulative.

One of the most effective elements with which to help dissolve this inorganic, incrustated calcium has been found in grapefruit, in its organic salicylic acid content. Thus, one pint or more of fresh grapefruit juice daily helps to dissolve this accumulation of foreign matter. The canned juice has usually been found useless for this purpose.

Oil of wintergreen has highly penetrating ethers and contains a high percentage of salicylic acid. It is often used externally to help ease the pain which usually follows the cleansing and regeneration of the cartilage and the joints.

Dissolving the inorganic calcium, however, is only the first step in the progressive course of this regeneration. It is so difficult to acknowledge RESENTMENTS and to banish them, but this is the very first step necessary to help to improve the situation. The calcium must be removed from the body, so we drink one pint daily of straight celery juice whose very high sodium content helps maintain the calcium more or less in solution. The blood and lymph both carry this waste matter toward the colon, and to facilitate the functions of that organ we drink one pint of carrot and spinach juice. This combination serves to nourish the nerves and muscles of the large and small intestines.

One pint of carrot and celery juice daily helps to rebuild and regenerate the cartilage and the joints, eventually helping to restore them to their normal state.

The process is usually painful—more so at certain times than at others; but we have seen many sufferers go through it and in time become more active than ever before. It requires will power and the cooperation of everybody interested in the victim's welfare, but the results have proved to be worth it.

Vaccines, drugs, heat, electricity, and a variety of orthodox nostrums have proved valueless as remedies. The elimination of pain does not cure the cause.

If the human body is suffering as a result of the transgression of the fundamental laws governing its nutrition, then cleansing the debris and waste from the system and nourishing it with the vital organic atoms of fresh raw vegetables and fruits, cannot help but restore at least some of the ebbing energy and vitality.

When such nourishment has been taken in the form of fresh raw juices properly extracted, the results have been speedier and more pronounced, once RESENT-MENTS have been dissolved from the consciousness.

LIST OF FORMULAS

Compiled by N. W. Walker, D.Sc., through the
Norwalk Laboratory of Nutritional Chemistry
and Scientific Research.

1. Carrot
2. Potassium (Carrot, Celery, Parsley and Spinach)
3. Beet and tops
4. Brussels Sprouts
5. Cabbage
6. Celery
7. Cucumber
8. Dandelion
9. Endive (Chicory)
10. Green Peppers
11. Horseradish and Lemon
12. Lettuce
13. Parsley
14. Radish and Tops
15. Spinach
16. String Beans
17. Turnip and Tops
18. Watercress
19. Alfalfa
20. Apple
21. Coconut
22. Grapefruit
23. Lemon
24. Orange
25. Pomegranate
26. Carrot and Beet

27. Carrot, Apple and Beet
28. Carrot, Beet and Celery
29. Carrot, Beet and Coconut
30. Carrot, Beet and Cucumber
31. Carrot, Beet and Lettuce
32. Carrot, Beet, Lettuce and Turnip
33. Carrot, Beet and Spinach
34. Carrot and Cabbage
35. Carrot, Cabbage and Celery
36. Carrot, Cabbage and Lettuce
37. Carrot and Celery
38. Carrot, Celery and Endive
39. Carrot, Celery and Lettuce
40. Carrot, Celery and Parsley
41. Carrot, Celery and Radish
42. Carrot, Celery and Spinach
43. Carrot, Celery and Turnip
44. Carrot and Cucumber
45. Carrot and Dandelion
46. Carrot, Dandelion and Lettuce
47. Carrot, Dandelion and Spinach
48. Carrot, Dandelion and Turnip
49. Carrot and Endive
50. Carrot, Celery, Endive and Parsley
51. Carrot and Green Peppers
52. Carrot and Lettuce
53. Carrot, Lettuce and Alfalfa
54. Carrot, Lettuce and Cucumber
55. Carrot, Lettuce and Spinach
56. Carrot, Lettuce and String Beans
57. Carrot, Lettuce, String Beans and Brussels Sprouts
58. Carrot, Lettuce and Turnip
59. Carrot and Parsley
60. Carrot and Radish
61. Carrot and Spinach

62. Carrot, Spinach, Turnip and Watercress
63. Carrot and Turnip
64. Carrot, Turnip and Watercress
65. Carrot and Watercress
66. Carrot and Alfalfa
67. Carrot and Apple
68. Carrot and Fennel
69. Carrot and Coconut
70. Grapefruit, Lemon and Orange
71. Carrot and Orange
72. Carrot and Pomegranate
73. Carrot, Beet and Pomegranate
74. Carrot, Lettuce and Pomegranate
75. Cabbage and Celery
76. Celery, Cucumber, Parsley and Spinach
77. Celery, Cucumber and Turnip
78. Celery, Dandelion and Spinach
79. Celery, Endive and Parsley
80. Celery, Lettuce and Spinach
81. Celery, Spinach and Parsley
82. Celery and String Beans
83. Brussels Sprouts and String Beans
84. Carrot, Brussels Sprouts and String Beans
85. Carrot, Asparagus and Lettuce
86. Carrot, Radish and Watercress
87. Carrot, Parsnip, Potato and Watercress

FORMULAS

The following Formulas are given entirely as a matter of courtesy by the Norwalk Laboratory of Nutritional Chemistry and Scientific Research for use with Special Vegetable Juice Equipment. They represent the result of expensive and laborious research by this Laboratory in Raw Vegetable Juice Therapy.

It is essential to bear in mind that satisfactory results from the use of these combinations have been obtained with juices made with the Electric Triturator and Hydraulic Press. Such equipment has been found to extract the Vitamins, Minerals and other Vital Elements from vegetables and fruits and to retain the Enzymes more completely than by any other method.

When any other type of Juice Extractor was used, it was found necessary to considerably increase the indicated quantity. Any juice, so long as it is fresh and raw, is better than no juice at all.

We belong to the kingdom next higher than that of the animals. We have a free will and the ability to use it and develop it. If man persists in the transgression of Nature's laws, Providence steps in to save him from annihilation, if possible.

Our fundamental object and goal in life should be to gain vast and abundant knowledge, and learn to apply it intelligently. Of what value is life, let alone longevity, unless we live intelligently?

We can teach Wisdom, but we cannot make one learn Wisdom. If it is too much trouble to learn how to attain and maintain health, and to put such knowledge into practice, then the easier way out is to follow the line of least resistance and hope fervently that the grave is not too far away.

Whether or not you have studied anatomy and the physiology of its functions, it is always best to have a doctor who has had personal experience with Raw Vegetable Juices to check your condition and consult him in regard to it. If you have studied carefully all the preceding pages, your own conviction and intelligence should help you to follow the course of Natural Healing which has been so consistently helpful to others.

Where individual juices are indicated, there is naturally no need for a FORMULA PROPORTION. Where Formula Numbers are not included in the following enumeration they are single individual juices.

FORMULA PROPORTIONS found to be consistently helpful when used in the COMBINATIONS and PROPORTIONS indicated, are listed below.

The NUMBERS of INDIVIDUAL juices are listed on the preceding pages.

One Pint—16 Ounces

#2 Carrot   7 oz.
    Celery   4 oz.
    Parsley   2 oz.
    Spinach   3 oz.

#11 Juice 1 whole
    lemon to ¼ pt.
    (4 oz.) Horse-
    radish ground
    but not pressed.

#26 Carrot   13 oz.
    Beet   3 oz.
    Note: Use beet
    tops and roots.

#27 Carrot   7 oz.
    Apple   6 oz.
    Beet   3 oz.

#28 Carrot   8 oz.
    Beet   3 oz.
    Celery   5 oz.

#29 Carrot   11 oz.
    Beet   3 oz.
    Coconut   2 oz.

#30 Carrot   10 oz.
    Beet   3 oz.
    Cucumber   3 oz.

#31 Carrot   9 oz.
    Beet   3 oz.
    Lettuce   4 oz.

#32 Carrot   7 oz.
    Beet   3 oz.
    Lettuce   4 oz.
    Turnip   2 oz.

#33 Carrot   10 oz.
    Beet   3 oz.
    Spinach   3 oz.

#34 Carrot   11 oz.
    Cabbage   5 oz.

#35 Carrot   7 oz.
    Cabbage   4 oz.
    Celery   5 oz.

#36 Carrot   8 oz.
    Cabbage   4 oz.
    Lettuce   4 oz.

#37 Carrot   9 oz.
    Celery   7 oz.
    Note: If celery
    tops (greens) are
    used, then change
    the proportion to
    10 oz. Carrot,
    6 oz. Celery.

#38 Carrot   9 oz.
    Celery   5 oz.
    Endive
    (Escarole) 2 oz.

#39 Carrot   7 oz.
    Celery   5 oz.
    Lettuce   4 oz.

#40 Carrot	9 oz.
Celery	5 oz.
Parsley	2 oz.

#41 Carrot	8 oz.
Celery	5 oz.
Radish	3 oz.

#42 Carrot	7 oz.
Celery	5 oz.
Spinach	4 oz.

#43 Carrot	8 oz.
Celery	6 oz.
Turnip	2 oz.

| #44 Carrot | 12 oz. |
| Cucumber | 4 oz. |

| #45 Carrot | 12 oz. |
| Dandelion | 4 oz. |

#46 Carrot	9 oz.
Dandelion	3 oz.
Lettuce	4 oz.

#47 Carrot	10 oz.
Dandelion	3 oz.
Spinach	3 oz.

#48 Carrot	11 oz.
Dandelion	3 oz.
Turnip	2 oz.

#49 Carrot	13 oz.
Endive	
(Escarole)	3 oz.

#50 Carrot	7 oz.
Celery	5 oz.
Endive	
(Escarole)	2 oz.
Parsley	2 oz.

#51 Carrot	12 oz.
Green	
Peppers	4 oz.

| #52 Carrot | 10 oz. |
| Lettuce | 6 oz. |

#53 Carrot	9 oz.
Lettuce	4 oz.
Alfalfa	3 oz.

#54 Carrot	7 oz.
Lettuce	5 oz.
Cucumber	4 oz.

#55 Carrot	8 oz.
Lettuce	5 oz.
Spinach	3 oz.

#56 Carrot	9 oz.
Lettuce	4 oz.
String Beans	3 oz.

#57 Carrot	6 oz.
Lettuce	4 oz.
String Beans	3 oz.
Brus. Sprouts	3 oz.

#58 Carrot	10 oz.
Lettuce	4 oz.
Turnip	2 oz.

| #59 Carrot | 12 oz. |
| Parsley | 4 oz. |

| #60 Carrot | 11 oz. |
| Radish | 5 oz. |

| #61 Carrot | 10 oz. |
| Spinach | 6 oz. |

#62 Carrot	8 oz.
Spinach	4 oz.
Turnip	2 oz.
Watercress	2 oz.

| #63 Carrot | 12 oz. |
| Turnip | 4 oz. |

#64 Carrot	10 oz.
Turnip	3 oz.
Watercress	3 oz.

| #65 Carrot | 12 oz. |
| Watercress | 4 oz. |

| #66 Carrot | 12 oz. |
| Alfalfa | 4 oz. |

#67 Carrot	9 oz.		#78 Celery	8 oz.
Apple	7 oz.		Dandelion	4 oz.
			Spinach	4 oz.
#68 Carrot	9 oz.			
Fennel	7 oz.		#79 Celery	11 oz.
			Endive	
#69 Carrot	13 oz.		(Escarole)	3 oz.
Coconut	3 oz.		Parsley	2 oz.
#70 Grapefruit	6 oz.		#80 Celery	7 oz.
Lemon	3 oz.		Lettuce	5 oz.
Orange	7 oz.		Spinach	4 oz.
#71 Carrot	11 oz.		#81 Celery	10 oz.
Orange	5 oz.		Spinach	4 oz.
			Parsley	2 oz.
#72 Carrot	11 oz.			
Pomegranate	5 oz.		#82 Celery	12 oz.
			String Beans	4 oz.
#73 Carrot	9 oz.			
Beet	3 oz.		#83 Brus. Sprouts	7 oz.
Pomegranate	4 oz.		String Beans	9 oz.
#74 Carrot	7 oz.		#84 Carrot	6 oz.
Lettuce	5 oz.		Brus. Sprouts	5 oz.
Pomegranate	4 oz.		String Beans	5 oz.
#75 Cabbage	5 oz.		#85 Carrot	8 oz.
Celery	11 oz.		Asparagus	4 oz.
			Lettuce	4 oz.
#76 Celery	8 oz.			
Cucumber	3 oz.		#86 Carrot	8 oz.
Parsley	2 oz.		Radish	4 oz.
Spinach	3 oz.		Watercress	4 oz.
			#87 Carrot	6 oz.
#77 Celery	10 oz.		Parsnip	4 oz.
Cucumber	4 oz.		Potato	4 oz.
Turnip	2 oz.		Watercress	2 oz.

NOTE: Use Tops AND Roots of Beets, Dandelion, Radish and Turnips.

When preparing Carrots cut off the tops ½ inch below the ring where the green stems start and snip off the tail of the carrot.

To remove sprays, etc., we wash vegetables thoroughly with plenty of cold, running water, using a stiff brush when necessary.

Certain prevailing laws require that contagious and infectious ailments be treated under the direction of a doctor. Whenever possible, we would seek a Doctor who is familiar with the benefits which are derived from colon irrigations AND the use of fresh raw vegetable and fruit juices and diet, instead of drugs, serums and "shots."

AILMENTS AND FORMULAS

NOTE: It is not legal to diagnose and prescribe anything whatever in case of illness except by a Doctor Licensed to do so. The following AILMENTS and corresponding FORMULAS are listed here as a guide for the HEALING PROFESSION and are given for their general information. While they are based on past experience, they are not intended to be used as prescriptions. These FORMULAS are the result of extensive research done by this Author with the cooperation of R. D. Pope, M.D.

The detailed list of the indicated FORMULAS will be found on preceding pages.

ACIDOSIS: The toxic condition of the 61 30 body, usually the result of the retention of waste and corrupt matter in the colon, the natural result of an orthodox diet consisting mainly of concentrated starches, sugars and meat. The use of bicarbonate of soda to relieve this condition is unwise and shortsighted, as this inorganic material may in course of time lodge in the region of the brain and damage it. It then may manifest as a silvergray crescent in the upper part of the iris of the eye. To help correct acidosis, read chapter on Spinach Juice, page 80. Acidosis may also result from mental disturbances such as resentments, worry, anger, fear, jealousy, frustration, etc. The first prerequisite to help clear up this condition is to develop a placid mind and to learn to RELAX!

ACNE, Pimples, etc., Impurities in the body trying to be eliminated through the skin. One of the manifestations of acidosis. We would refrain from using salves and ointments, drugs of any kind, and X ray, using instead natural methods to remove the cause.

61 1 55

ADDISON'S DISEASE: The result of lack of vital organic sodium principally, and an excess of waste matter in the system generally, affecting the adrenal glands. The injection of extracts from the glands of dead cattle cannot cure this condition. We have, however, seen much benefit derived from a high sodium and low potassium raw diet rigidly adhered to: Romaine lettuce is particularly beneficial. See chapter on this vegetable on page 69.

3 6
12
(Romaine lettuce only)
25 74 80

ADENOIDS: Inflammation or enlargement of pharyngeal, tonsil, or adenoid tissue, due to excessive mucus in the system and waste matter in the lower intestines, as a result of drinking cow's milk and eating too many starchy and sugary foods.

61 1

ALBUMINURIA: Albumin present in the urine.

61 30 29 1
40 59

ALLERGY: The physical discomfort or irritation due to excessive retention of waste in the system when food is eaten which has the effect of stirring up toxins in the body. Allergy to strawberries, for

61 30 1

133

example, means that this fruit may stir up poisons which manifest themselves, sometimes, as hives.

ANEMIA: Deficiency of red blood corpuscles or of the red coloring matter of the blood, caused by prolonged habit of eating foods in which the calcium and other atoms have been devitalized, such as canned foods, starches, and pasteurized milk. The use of liver extract, whether orally or by injection, was once upon a time considered a cure; due to the damage these extracts do to the kidneys, many victims were found to develop Bright's disease sooner or later.

61 68   2 28
30 25 29 31
46 55 48 85

ANGINA PECTORIS: Valvular or muscular heart trouble resulting from impurities in the blood stream, but frequently found to be the result of gas pressure in the colon.

61   2 30

APHONIA: Loss of the power of articulation in speech.

61   1 48 53

APOPLEXY: Stroke of paralysis, the result of blood pressure in the brain, caused by impurities in the blood vessels—such, for example, as the inorganic calcium from eating excessive amounts of starches and rich foods over a period of years. Impactions in the lower intestines, with the consequent absorption of toxins from these, have been found to be one of the contributing causes. Repeated enemas, daily, and a strictly fresh raw diet with at least 2 quarts of juices daily have proved of inestimable value.

61 62   2 28
39

APPENDICITIS: Inflammation of the appendix resulting from the excessive accumulation and retention of waste matter in the colon. The appendix is a gland, the secretion of which is intended to neutralize excessive putrefaction and pathogenic bacterial action in the colon, or large intestine, which might have injurious repercussion in the small, or digestive intestine. To avoid unnecessary surgery, satisfactory results have been obtained by colonic irrigations, where available, and high enemas in any case, at 15 to 30 minute intervals, until the elimination of waste matter removed danger and pain. Consult a doctor familiar with Nature's purpose in furnishing us with this protective gland.

1 2 30 61

ARTERIES, ARTERIOSCLEROSIS, etc.: The result of deficiency of vital organic calcium and excess of inorganic calcium in the diet causing the blood vessels to lose elasticity and causing blood to coagulate in the veins. Inorganic calcium deposits convert the elastic walls of blood vessels into solid tubes. Nature alone can remedy this condition, but only with the utmost and unreserved cooperation of the victim.

61 2 80 28
55

ARTHRITIS: Inorganic calcium deposits in the cartilage of the joints as a result of eating concentrated carbohydrates in excess. See special chapter on this subject.

22 61 6 37
30

ASTHMA: Extreme difficulty in breathing due to mucus accumulation in the bronchial tubes. Victims who have followed Nature's principles have had no difficulty in relieving themselves of this punishment for eating and drinking mucus-forming

61 11 37 60
41

135

foods. Once relieved completely of asthma, one can readily get it back again, if he so desires, by simply eating plenty of white bread, dairy products and drinking plenty of cow's milk. In fact, almost any kind of concentrated carbohydrates and dairy products, cheese, etc., will oblige by inviting this enemy to return. Allergy tests, drug panaceas, blood and sputum studies, and environment investigations are as a rule extremely useful—in making matters worse. The CAUSE of asthma is the presence of mucus. Read the chapter on Horseradish.

ASTIGMATISM: A disfunction in vision 1 61 30 50
due to the imperfect condition of the eye as a result of vital organic atoms lacking in the nourishment of the optic system, accentuated by the presence of waste matter in the organs and glands directly affecting the eyes. The liver, the gall bladder, the pancreas, the thyroid, and the colon are all glands and organs whose inefficient operation is a direct contributing factor in any disfunction of the optic system.

ATHLETE'S FOOT: The banquet of ring- 61 30 1
worms, particularly between the toes where the piece-de-resistance is acidity collecting in our lower extremities when our feet are deprived of their breathing. Ringworms are wonderful hosts, collecting guests wherever they can, so long as the acidity of the feet is kept inside solid leather shoes preventing the dissipation of the acid toxins. The answer to their eviction lies in the ventilation as much as possible of the feet. Sandals are being used more and more in appreciation of their beneficial effect, not only for the

feet, but for the entire anatomy. Rainy weather, and frequently snow, have been found less harmful when wearing sandals than when wearing shoes and rubbers.

BACKACHE: This may result from innu- 61 30 1 2
merable causes. The safest thing to do is to see a good osteopath or chiropractor who understands Natural methods as well as mechanical adjustments of the spine. He should be able to determine whether it results from lumbago, from constipation, or from spinal or cranial maladjustments.

BED-WETTING: This habit in children 30
should disappear during the first or second year. When persistent, omit fluids after, say, 4:00 p.m., but give plenty during the day. Watch approximately the time wetting takes place, wake up the child on following nights about 10 to 20 minutes before that time, and continue practice until child functions voluntarily. Cooked spinach and rhubarb are probably the best foods to prolong bed-wetting as the inorganic oxalic acid crystals may irritate the kidneys and these become overactive.

BILIOUSNESS: The result of incomplete 61 30 40
digestion of fats and excessive fermentation in the system, causing improper secretion and flow of bile from the liver. Alcoholic liquors, including beer, degenerating the liver, have the tendency to chronically disorganize the digestive functions. Fried and fatty food are the most frequent cause of biliousness.

BLADDER TROUBLE: Irritations in this 30 61
organ are usually the result of excessive

acidity accumulating as a result of eating foods leaving acid end products insufficiently digested or discolved—uric acid crystals, for example, from eating meat, and oxalie acid crystals from using cooked spinach or rhubarb. Allowing these crystals to accumulate, and persisting in eating such foods, may cause growths to form. The removal of these growths by burning, cutting, X ray, radium, and drugs does not remove the cause. On the contrary, the eventual return of even more serious conditions is likely to follow. Excessive use of concentrated starches is also a contributory cause. Inflammation of the bladder may interfere with the normal flow of urine, causing damage to the walls of the bladder. Cystitis is the name given to this condition.

Bladder stones may either form within the bladder or may have been passed from the kidneys. See Kidney Stones. Much bladder trouble in men is due also to trouble with the prostate gland.

BLINDNESS: See Cataracts. Read also chapter on Endive Juice.

BLOOD PRESSURE, HIGH: The result of **61   2 30 15** impurities in the blood vessels. The only way impurities can get into the blood stream is (1) by hypodermic injections and drugs, whether taken as medicine or otherwise; (2) by deposits in the blood stream of inorganic atoms accumulating from cooked and processed foods, particularly the concentrated starches and sugars; and (3) by retention of waste in the eliminative organs and channels.

The recurrence of high blood pressure within families is not due to heredity, as erroneously supposed by some, unless we consider the degenerated condition of the mother's blood stream (due to eating inorganic foods) as her hereditary gift to her child. The only hereditary trait is the kind and quality of the food the family as a whole habitually indulges in; if this contains an excessive proportion of cooked foods and concentrated carbohydrates, it is only natural that a nutritional deficiency should manifest itself in most, if not in all of its members.

BLOOD PRESSURE, LOW: Primarily due to nutritional deficiency as a result of eating all or mostly cooked and processed foods, and in any case as a rule because of the absence from the diet of fresh raw vegetable juices which can be quickly and efficiently used in the regeneration of the blood corpuscles. One very serious contributing cause is the lack of proper and sufficient rest. Each hour's sleep before 10:00 p.m. is worth more than two hours' sleep in the morning.

61   2 30   1
29 15

Smoking and alcoholic drinks are paramount reasons for high and low blood pressures.

BOILS: Purulent or pus-filled tumors caused by impurities in the blood stream resulting in bacterial infection through the sweat glands or the follicles of the hair. The use of sulfa and other drugs may have dangerous repercussions.

61 30 55

A boil is not an infection of the skin, but simply waste matter which the body has been unable to throw off through other eliminative channels, either because these are impacted with the accumulation of waste, or because they have degenerated into inactivity through lack of proper nourishment and attention. When the body fails to eliminate waste matter through the main eliminative organs, then the greatest eliminative system of the body is called upon to help. This system is the skin and its pores.

BOTULISM: Food poisoning resulting **15 66** from the deadly poison of the gas given off by the botulinus germ while it is being slowly killed by heat, much in the same manner that a skunk ejects a well-known fluid when irritably disturbed. It is a deadly poison frequently present in canned foods when insufficient heat has not completely destroyed them. It is also likely to be present in sausages, meat, and fish pastes. When afflicted, call your doctor and notify the undertaker. Fresh raw vegetable juices are live foods intended for live people.

BRAIN TUMORS: The result of impurities **62 61 30 40** in the blood stream coagulating in the blood vessels of the brain. They cause pressure inside the skull, resulting usually in disfunction of speech and thought, or of body movement, according to the location of the tumor. Surgery causes the death of about 50% of its victims while colonic irrigations or enemas and other cleansing processes are overlooked.

BRONCHITIS: Inflammation of the bron- **61 45 11 30** chial tubes due to excessive mucus in the **1 37 60 41** system. It is one of Nature's means to warn us of this excessive accumulation of waste in the body, and when the warning is ignored Nature may raise the body temperature to fever heat to burn up this debris. If we continue to disregard this warning and fail to cleanse our insides

pretty thoroughly, Nature will furnish us
with germs and bacteria to do the scavenging which may result in further discomforts such as colds, influenza, or
pneumonia. It has been absorbingly interesting to watch victims of these conditions recover speedily after taking sufficient colonic irrigations, high enemas,
and detoxication. Read the chaper on
Detoxication.

BURSITIS: The result of the drying up of 86 30 61
the Synovial lubricating fluid in the
joints. Some avocado eaten daily has
been helpful in eventually helping to restore normalcy.

1 61

CANCERS: Groups or nests of epithelial
cells half starved from lack of proper organic nourishment, thriving on concentrated starches and meats. Read the
chapter on Carrot Juice where a description of cancer is outlined.

One of the contributing factors, in my
opinion, in the development of cancer
has been found to be prolonged RE-
SENTMENTS.

CARBUNCLES: See Boils.

CATALEPSY: Muscular rigidity resulting 61 2 40 30
from improperly nourished nerves.

CATARACTS: Opaque films floating over 61 50 1 40
the crystalline lens of the eye due to lack 30
of proper nourishment to the optic nerves
and muscles. While surgery has been of
temporary benefit in some cases, there is
no question that Nature can work greater
and more permanent benefits than even
the most skillful of men, provided that

the one affected cooperates wholeheartedly. Read the chapter on Endive Juice.

CATARRH: Copious secretions from the 61 11 30 41 mucous membrane due to the inability of 60 the body properly to assimilate milk and concentrated starches.

CHICKEN POX: The chicken pox virus 61 30 1 2 propagates in a medium of mucus, particularly that which results from the waste of the digestion of milk and concentrated starches and sugars. In the absence of such medium, naturally the virus cannot exist; but if the child is brought up on cow's milk, cereals, breads, and puddings, it is only to be expected that this microscopic virus—which must eat if it is to live—will propagate in such fertile soil. A virus is a living pathogenic micro-organism. No living thing can continue to live without food. If the chicken pox virus does not happen to appreciate the particular quality of the mucus present, then Nature will oblige by furnishing some other virus or germ to do the scavenging, and, depending on the name given to this scavenger, another one of the so-called "natural diseases of childhood" may "develop." A diet of starches, grains, and milk is fine for the germ, as also are the ointments so frequently used, as these drive the poisons back into the skin, and so into the body, to reappear at some early or distant date under some other classification. Iris diagnosis has done more to prove this than all laboratory methods we have been able to find. The same treatment which has been so effectively used in colds (which see) has been efficacious in cases of chicken pox.

CHOREA (or St. Vitus' Dance): Detoxication (which see) as a first step, has given excellent results when followed with an entirely raw diet of fresh vegetables, fruits, and nuts.   **61 2 30 40**

CIRRHOSIS of the Liver: The direct effect of overworking the liver as a result of eating too many starches, particularly white flour, causing the liver tissues to harden.   **1 61 30**

COLDS: Same as catarrh (which see), but in a less virulent or tenacious form. Colonic irrigations or high enemas have proved of primary benefit in ridding the body of colds. When possible, a three-day detoxication was carried out with amazingly satisfactory results. Read chapter on Detoxication. The prevention of colds is without doubt the simplest thing in creation. Once we have gone through the arduous and bothersome process of cleansing the body of mucus and other waste matter, and have changed to the mucusless diet of raw vegetables and fruits (see DIET & SALAD book by N. W. Walker, D.Sc.) supplemented with plenty of fresh juices, the cause of colds is removed. Read once again the brief but significant paragraphs immediately preceded by the heading AILMENTS AND FORMULAS. Vaccines, drugs, and hypodermic injections are exceedingly profitable to those who administer them, and it is even within the range of possibility that some of these persons may not know that they are of no ultimate benefit whatever.   **61 11 30 41** 60 23 (in hot water)

Read again the chapter with the heading: OH—SO, YOU HAVE A COLD?

COLIC: Gas pains in the abdominal re-   **61 30**

gions usually due to improper combinations of foods, and to the retention of waste matter in the system. Infants brought up on raw foods and juices rarely have colic. We have found that enemas help to give more or less instant relief.

COLITIS: Inflammation of the colon re- sulting from constipation, and from mental or organic nervousness which, of course, disrupts the digestive processes. The primary cause may usually be traced to the lack of organic live nourishment for the proper functioning of the colon. (Read chapter on Oxalic Acid and on Spinach.) Cooked food is composed of dead atoms which cannot nourish or regenerate any of the cells and tissues of the body. Cold buttermilk has been used to soothe the inflamed tissues of the colon while a change-over to a properly prepared raw food diet was in progress; but we must remember that all milk is mucus-forming, so that if it is used in an emergency, it must be used judiciously. It has been found that cooked foods, instead of helping to re-establish normalcy in the colon, have the opposite effect. Finely grated carrots and other vegetables and fruits similarly prepared, all raw, have been of great help when properly made fresh, raw juices were also used plentifully. Mineral oils, being inorganic, defeat any attempt to benefit the condition, while drugs are injurious to the system. High enemas have proved of immense benefit. The objection to enemas usually comes from those who need them most but are not sufficiently informed on the subject of nutritional and eliminative physiology. The fear that they are habit-forming is based on lack of knowledge. Cleanliness—whether internal or external —is never harmful.

CONJUNCTIVITIS: Inflammation of the membranes of the eye.   61 50   1 59

CONSTIPATION: A colon filled with tox- 61 15 30   1
ins, resulting in lack of coordination in the nerve and muscle functions of the colon and bowel due to excessive use of devitalized foods in the diet, resulting in sluggishness of bowel action. Be sure to read carefully the chapters on Spinach Juice and Oxalic Acid.

CORONARY THROMBOSIS: See Throm- 11 61 30
bosis.

COUGHING: The result of the body try- ing to dislodge and rid itself of mucus from the breathing passages. Cough med- icines are mostly an excellent means to store up a future supply of coughs, and are intended for the gullible. Read the paragraph on Colds. Gargling the throat with the juice of lemons, straight or dilut- ed, has helped to ease up a cough.

CRAMPS: In the intestinal region. Pains 61 30
due to the presence of gas resulting from foods improperly combined.
In the muscles. Usually due to excessive retention of uric acid.

CYSTITIS: Inflammation of the urinary 30 61 40 29
bladder. See paragraph on Bladder Trou- 51
ble.

DEAFNESS: Frequently due to the pres- 61 11 40 41
ence of mucus in the auditory channels. Sometimes due to cranial pressure on the

nerves and blood vessels related to the auditory system. Cranial adjustments, known as Craniopathy, usually relieve this condition.

DECAY (of bone): Decomposition of bone tissue due to excessive use of milk and concentrated starches and sugars in the diet.
61 48 55 46 1

DECAY (of teeth): Decomposition due to the lack of organic live atoms in the food to nourish the teeth. Excessive use of milk, starches, and sugars are primary causes of decay.
61 48 55 46 1

DIABETES: Inability of the pancreas to metabolize carbohydrates due to excessive use of concentrated starches and sugars in the diet. Read chapter on String Bean Juice regarding injections of Insulin.
61 2 57 50 40 84 55

DIARRHEA: Loose running of the bowels. Usually Nature cleansing the colon because you failed to do so when you should.
1 2

DIPHTHERIA: A disease resulting from the settlement and propagation, usually in the throat, of the diphtheria germ, most common after the removal of tonsils. The feeding ground of the germ is the accumulation of body waste due to its improper elimination from the body and of unassimilable devitalized foods, principally starches, encumbering the blood stream. A clean pure body and blood stream cannot harbor diphtheria germs. To pollute such a body with diphtheria poison known as antitoxin and to inject
61 2 40 30 47

this poison into a body suspected of entertaining diphtheria germs, without first using natural cleansing and preventive means in the way of proper organic nourishment, is due to a singular lack of the elementary understanding of the purpose of germs in Nature.

DIZZINESS: The result of the body getting out of balance because of the accumulation of waste matter in the system. Read the chaper on Detoxication. It has helped many to get over their dizziness.   30 61   2   1

DROPSY: Excessive water in the system due to improper or insufficient elimination through the kidneys.   61 30 29 40
59 11

DYSENTERY: A loose running of the bowels as a result of an accumulation of mucus and other waste matter. Colonic irrigations, and sometimes a detoxication (already described), have been of great help when drinking two or three quarts of fresh juices a day.   6 61 30   1

DYSPEPSIA: Indigestion due to excessive acidity in the alimentary tract.   61   1   2 30
15

DYSURIA: Painful incomplete urination.   30   1 40 59

ECZEMA: Inflammatory condition of the skin due to excessive acidity of the lymph glands. Also, the elimination through the pores of the skin of waste matter which should really pass out through the kidneys and the bowels. Read the paragraph on Boils.   61   2 30 15

ELEPHANTIASIS: Inflammation and obstruction of the lymphatic glands usually   61 30 32
40

147

because of the presence of inorganic waste in the system.

EMPHYSEMA: (The word means "to in- 87 flate.") A condition resulting from an excess of air or gas in the tissues, usually in the lungs, or the presence of air or gas in normally airless tissues.

ENCEPHALITIS: Inflammation of the 61 30 40 37 brain as a result of a disturbed or unhealthy condition of the nerve system. Two ounces of parsley juice three times daily morning, noon and night and repeated enemas, together with the indicated juices have proved beneficial.

ENURESIS: Incontinence of urine, fre- 30 40 29 quently due to the presence of inorganic oxalic acid crystals in the kidneys or bladder. See chapter on Oxalic Acid.

EPILEPSY: Nervous spasms resulting from 61 15 2 30 excessive toxemia and starvation of the 40 nervous system. It is sometimes caused by the presence of worms in the colon. One such instance was that of a young woman about 26 years of age. After the 28th consecutive daily colonic irrigation, a mass of worms as large as a man's fist passed out. A few more colonics made a clean sweep of them, and her epileptic fits never recurred. This may have been a coincidence, but many more such cases were definitely educational.

ERYSIPELAS: Same as Eczema but accom- 61 2 30 40 panied by fever. The cause of both is the same.

EYE TROUBLE: See paragraph on Cata- 1 61 50 racts and read chapter on Endive Juice.

FATIGUE: An indication that the cells of the body are not getting sufficient live atoms in the food to furnish the constant flow of new energy needed. Fatigue is one of the precursors of disease. The cumulative effect is the destruction of tissue cells and the consequent accumulation of waste in the body; if not removed, this will be scavenged by germs and bacteria. Rest, sleep, cleansing of the colon, and plenty of juices have been found to be the best method to overcome fatigue.

1 61 30

FATTY DEGENERATION: Excessive formation of fatty cells and tissues around an organ.

61 15 30 42

FEVER: The name orthodoxically given to body temperature which rises above normal when Nature attempts to burn up or incinerate waste matter in the system. When there is no excessive waste matter and the body cells are properly nourished, there is no need for fever. It has been found repeatedly that by detoxicating (see chapter on Detoxication) and by the use of high enemas the fevered condition has been alleviated within an amazingly short time.

22 23 24

GALL BLADDER TROUBLE and GALLSTONES: Cooked fats and fried foods are the most common cause of a disorganized gall bladder function, regarding which see paragraph on Biliousness. Gallstones and gravel, however, are the accumulation of inorganic calcium and other inorganic matter collecting in the gall bladder due to the inability of the system to assimilate them. All starch, bread and grain products are full of such inorganic calcium. Eating plenty of these may tend

30 61 40 29 23

(in glass of hot water)

149

to furnish a plentiful crop of gallstones and gravel. The juice of a lemon in a glass of hot water, without sweetening, taken several times a day for 3 or 4 weeks has helped to dissolve these stones, when the other juices indicated herein were used daily over the same period of time. Nature never intended that man's gall bladder be removed by an operation. The gall bladder is essential to the proper functioning of the liver. Our body is our own, however, and if we are, through ignorance of its functioning, ready and willing to submit it to the practicing of surgery, there is no one we can blame but ourselves.

GASTRITIS: Distress due to excessive formation of gas in the system as a result of the improper combination of foods. All flour, grain, and sugar products may have a tendency to cause gastritis, and alcohol may do it quicker than any of these. Hot condiments, consisting of hot peppers, mustard, vinegar, tobacco, etc., are also responsible for this condition. Raw foods, grated or chopped as finely as possible, have been found repeatedly to be more beneficial than cooked foods. 61 15 30

GLANDS: Every gland in the body has a definite relation to every other gland, either stimulating it, inhibiting it or in some way or another exercising a controlling influence on it. Read carefully the chapter on a preceding page, entitled YOUR ENDOCRINE GLANDS. Understand the influence of the various Glands on one another. It would be foolish for anyone to have a "Gland Operation" without realizing what effect this would have on the rest of the body. It would also be wise to learn how to nourish the glands so that a complete balance may be established between them. Learn about the mineral and chemical elements composing the glands and the juices which have been found to be most efficient in nourishing them. Send for a copy of the ENDO-CRINE GLAND CHART alluded to in the preceding chapter above referred to, frame it, and hang it where it can be studied constantly. It has saved many an unnecessary operation.

GOITER: Enlargement of the thyroid gland due to lack of organic iodine in the diet. The use of chemical iodine, and chemically prepared potassium iodide, is detrimental to the system as they are inorganic, and may sooner or later result in deposits which may cause damage to tissues in the body. The finest organic iodine is found in dulse, sea lettuce, and kelp. (See chapter on Seaweed.)

61 59 2
(with the addition of ¼ teaspoon of Powdered Kelp, Sea Lettuce or Dulse)

GONORRHEA: The result of the propagation of the gonococcus germ due to an impure blood stream and the presence of morbid matter as its feeding ground in the body, usually centering in the region of the genitals. Physicians in France have found that Sandalwood Oil in soluble capsules has proved of much benefit.

61 15 30 40 76 59

GOUT: Inflammation of the ligaments of a joint or bone, or bone lining, due to excessive fat in the diet; also due to excessive use of alcohol and other stimulants. Gout and rheumatism are almost identical twins.

61 2 30 29 15 40 59

GRAVEL: Inorganic matter, principally

30 40 59

151

the calcium of breads and other concen- 23
trated starches, forming granular secre- (in glass of
tions in the kidneys. hot water)

HAIR: Read the Chapter on ALFALFA 53 66
JUICE.

HALITOSIS: This word means "bad 61
breath." It results from the retention of
fermented and putrified food waste in the
body. The decay of teeth and so-called
infection of tissues is purely coincidental,
also resulting from such retention of
waste. Detoxication removes such waste
matter.

HAY FEVER: Abnormal secretions of 61 11 30 40
mucus in the eyes, nose, and air passages 15 50 41
due to the excessive use of milk, starches,
and grain products. We have found that
it is much more constructive to avoid hypodermic injections than it is to avoid
fresh air. See paragraph on Asthma,
which applies equally to Hay Fever.

HEADACHES: Any one of more than 200 61 2 30 55
manifestations that the body is overload- 15
ed with waste matter. Nature's warning
to give the body a thorough cleansing,
thus reestablishing the equilibrium of the
blood and releasing its excessive pressure
in the region of the head.

HEART-BURN: See PYROSIS.

HEART TROUBLE: Usually results from 61 2 30
impurities clogging up the blood vessels
which in turn place an excessive strain on
the heart. After all, the heart is only
about the size of one's fist, it weighs only
about 10 ounces, but nevertheless pumps
6 ounces of blood every time it contracts.

This does not seem much, but cumulatively it amounts to about 5,000 gallons every 24 hours under normal conditions. Under stress, however, this volume may reach as high as 25,000 gallons in 24 hours. During the normal sedentary lifetime of threescore years and ten there would be about 3,000,000,000 (three billion) heartbeats, with an added 30% for so-called stress and strain during that period. No man-made mechanism could carry on day in and day out without completely disintegrating within a very short time if it did not get any better care than we give to our heart and the rest of our body.

The blood carries everything it picks up in the system, through the heart. Thus the starch molecules of bread and flour and of grain products, not being soluble in water, have a tendency to clog up the blood stream. In such a condition it places an excessive strain on the pumping mechanism of the heart, and trouble results. Gas pressure in the region of the Splenic Flexure on the left-hand side of the transverse colon has been known to be the contributing factor in heart trouble. My FOOT RELAXATION CHART has assisted many students to be helpful in such conditions.

HEMORRHOIDS (Piles): The coagulation 62 61 2 of blood fibrin in the dead-ends of blood vessels in the lower part of the rectum as a result of eating too much bread and other starch and grain products. Their removal by means of a knife or electric needle is an excellent indoor sport for all except the patient. Their recurrence is almost inevitable sooner or later, when so removed, so long as the cause itself, namely the waste matter in the blood stream, is not properly taken care of.

HERNIA: Protrusion of any internal organ wholly or in part from its normal position, due to lack of tone in the surrounding membranes. 61 1 2 15 30

HIGH BLOOD PRESSURE: Excessive tension of the blood in the arteries caused by improper diet. See paragraph, "BLOOD PRESSURE, HIGH."

HIVES: Same as Urticaria, which see.

HODGKIN'S DISEASE: Swelling of the lymph glands and the tonsils directly associated with a disturbance of the spleen, the result of deficiency in, and unbalance of the diet. There is rarely any hope after X ray or radium are used because the ultimate effect of these is beyond the control of man, as are also radioactive materials. Detoxication, a rigid, properly balanced and prepared raw food diet, and the necessary fresh juices have been found to give satisfactory results. 61 27 29 46

IMPOTENCE: Deficiency in propagative ability in the sex act. 15 1 30 27 40 31 59

INDIGESTION: The result of the improper digestion of incompatible foods. It also results from eating while under the stress and strain of worry, fear, or anxiety. 23 (in glass of hot water) 61 1 30 15

INFANTILE PARALYSIS: Also labeled Poliomyelitis. Not as serious and common a disease as the publicity of it would have us believe. The virus causing this disease cannot exist in healthy tissue. 61 40 32 1 2

154

Once it has obtained a foothold, the logical step is to starve it by destroying and removing from the body all the waste matter that would enable it to survive. Read the chapter on Detoxication. In any case, prevention lies in the proper nourishment consisting of live organic food which has not been cooked or processed. To reestablish the body to its normal condition this has been found to be equally as imperative. The use of drugs, by injection or otherwise, tends to delay progress as the cells and tissues cannot be nourished back to health thereby. I believe more infantile paralysis could probably be traced to the consumption of pasteurized milk, sugar, starches, cereals and to soft (carbonated) drinks than to any other cause.

INFLUENZA: Caused by excessive retention in the system of body and food waste resulting in a feeding and breeding ground for pathogenic bacteria, affecting principally the air passages but accompanied by fever and nervous prostration followed by great debility.

61 11 2 30
41 55

INSANITY: A derangement of the mental nervous system due to excessive toxins in the body and insufficient organic nourishment. Even more frequently the contributing factor has been found to emanate from excessive mental pressure resulting from fears, resentment and similar disturbances.

61 37 30 1
15 2 40 59

INSOMNIA: Inability to sleep as a result of nervous tension or excessive acidity in the system.

61 37 30 22

ITCH: An uncomfortable condition caused

61 30 15 1

by certain germs or bacteria attempting to leave the body by way of the pores of the skin, resulting in the formation of pustules and accompanied by intense itching.

JAUNDICE: The result of an overburdened liver eliminating the excretion of bile by way of the lymph stream through the pores of the skin. 61 30 29 40 1

KIDNEY TROUBLE (Excessive Uric Acid, etc.): The result of improper and insufficient elimination of the end-products of excessive use of meat in the diet. Beer, wines and liquor are primary factors in kidney trouble. 30 61 40 29 59

LARYNGITIS: Inflammation of the larynx due to the presence of morbid matter in the body. 61 1 30 15

LEUKEMIA: Excessively rapid increase of the white blood cells, causing the breakdown of red blood cells, as a result of insufficient organic atoms in the diet—too much cooked food, starches, sugar, and meat and not enough fresh juices, raw vegetables, and fruits. 1 26 48 53

LEUCORRHEA: Excessive formation or accumulation of mucus in the female genital organs and passages. 61 11 30 2 40 41 60 59

LIVER TROUBLE: The result of eating an excess of devitalized and concentrated starches, sugars, fats and meats. Beer, wines and liquors are also primary factors in liver disturbances. 30 61 1 29 40 46

LOW BLOOD PRESSURE: Due to excessive use of devitalized foods in the diet,

156

resulting in deficiency of vital elements in the blood stream. See paragraph, "BLOOD PRESSURE, LOW."

MALARIA FEVER: The pathological result of an impure blood and excessive retention of morbid matter in the body while in an atmosphere of foul or unwholesome air, enabling animal parasites, germs, and bacteria to thrive and propagate in the system.   61 11   1 30
41 15

    When the system has been saturated with quinine, atabrine or other drugs, we would detoxicate (see chapter on Detoxication) as often as necessary to rid the body of these drugs.

MASTOIDITIS: The result of mucus accumulations in the mastoid region of the skull behind the ear, causing inflammation. The best means to create a good dose of mastoiditis is to feed the child lots of cow's milk, particularly the pasteurized, and plenty of white bread, cereals, cake, and other flour foods. The best way to prevent it, we have found, is to avoid these. See paragraph under Colds.   61 32   2

MEASLES: Germs and bacteria surging out of the body through the skin. One of Nature's methods of housecleaning the system, particularly in childhood.   61   6 30   1
47

MELANCHOLIA: Toxic condition of the body and undernourished nerve system resulting in morbid brooding. Lack of self confidence.   61   7   2 30
15 37

MENINGITIS: The presence of the Meningococcus germ in the system because of the accumulation of waste matter on   61 30   2   1

157

which this germ thrives. When the body is healthy the germ perishes from lack of nourishment or passes on and out of the system, without affecting it.

MENOPAUSE: The penalty women pay for half a lifetime (40 to 50 years) of eating destructive foods which fail to nourish the blood and in fact any part of the system so that it can be rapidly and constantly regenerated. 61 32 73 30 2

MENSTRUATION: A study of the EN-DOCRINE GLANDS CHART already referred to may reveal one or more of the primary causes for disturbances in this connection. (See chapter on GLANDS.) 61 59 30 68 2

MIGRAINE: Impure blood stream and improperly nourished nerve centers causing intense ache usually on one side only of the head, dulling and depressing the individual. 61 2 30 15 47 37

MULTIPLE SCLEROSIS: Degenerative state of the nervous system due to starvation of nerve and cerebro-spinal cells. This disease is the most conclusive evidence of the destructive effect of starches and grains used as food for humans. No permanent improvement has ever been achieved, in my 50 years of observation, while the patient was allowed to eat bread, cereals and other starchy foods. Many people, however, have been helped slowly to recover, by omitting these, and meat, from the diet, eating instead mostly raw fruits and vegetables, drinking at least 3 quarts of fresh RAW juices daily, and with frequent colonic irrigations. The greatest danger in this disease comes from neglecting to follow this program 61 40 59 2 1 consistently, and so develop secondary complications.

NEPHRITIS: Inflammation of the kidneys usually resulting from an excessive retention of acid. (Read chapter on Protein in DIET & SALAD SUGGESTIONS.) 30 61 40 29 59

NERVOUSNESS: Irritability of certain nerve centers due to organic alkaline deficiency. 61 37 30 40 15

NEURALGIA: Intense pain in the region of a nerve which has been improperly nourished. 61 37 30 40

NEURASTHENIA: Functional depression of the nervous system due to improper and insufficient organic nourishment and materialized as a result of prolonged nervous strain, worry, anxiety, or overwork. 61 37 2 30 40 55

NEURITIS: The result usually of uric acid crystals pressing against muscles and nerves, causing intense pain. Eating meat is one of the primary causes of the presence of such excessive amounts of uric acid that the muscles become saturated with it, when it eventually forms into crystals. 23 30 61 40

NYMPHOMANIA: Abnormal sex appetite in women as a result of excessive use of condiments, alcohol, smoking or improper combination of foods. Occasionally due to functional disturbance and physical abnormalities of the organs, which are easily corrected. 61 2 30 15 29 40

OBESITY: Excessive adipose tissue resulting from incompatible combinations of 61 1 30 15 34 foods and eating excessive quantities of starches and sugars. Sometimes due to glandular disturbance. Study the chapter on GLANDS. We have the following interesting report from "Pavy on Food" about a Mr. Banting: After one year of eliminating from his diet all starchy and fatty foods, and all alcoholic beverages including beer, Mr. Banting lost 40 pounds in weight and 12 inches from his midriff. After 7 years he wrote: "I can conscientiously assert that I never lived so well as under the new plan of dietary which I should formerly have thought a dangerous, extravagant trespass upon health; I am very much better, bodily and mentally, pleased to believe that I hold the reins of health and comfort in my own hands."

ORCHITIS: Inflammation of Testes, due to excessive retention of morbid matter in the system, and sometimes to abuse. 30 61 40 25 37 59

OSTEOMYELITIS: The breaking down of the structure of the bone, usually accompanied by oozing of pus. The bone, like every other part of the body, requires live, organic nourishment. Without it, the cells starve, the waste matter accumulates, and the structure crumbles. 1 61 48 30 43

OXIDATION (Low): Lack of oxygen assimilation due to insufficient organic iron in the system. 61 30 37 46 55

PARALYSIS: Loss of power to control or coordinate the voluntary and involuntary muscles, due to starvation of the nerve centers. 61 40 30 6

PARALYSIS (Infantile): Inability of the

body to replenish and regenerate the spinal fluid due to improper metabolism, an excess of devitalized starches and sugars and a great deficiency in organic elements in the diet. Read Paragraph on INFANTILE PARALYSIS.

61 2 40 30
6 47

PARESIS: Functional inability of the cerebral nerves to coordinate, due to lack of proper organic nourishment.

61 30 40 15

PERITONITIS: Inflammation of the lining of the abdominal cavity.

61 2 30

PHLEBITIS: Inflammation of veins due to the presence of excessive quantities of starch-calcium and morbidity in the system.

PILES: (See Hemorrhoids.)

30 61 40

PLEURISY: Inflammation of the pleura due to the improper elimination of morbid matter from the body, usually accompanied with fever and pains when breathing.

61 30 11. 41

PNEUMONIA: Inflammation of the lung tissues due to the presence of abnormal quantities of mucus and other morbid matter in the system, as a result of drinking milk and the excessive use of concentrated starches and sugars.

POLIO: See INFANTILE PARALYSIS

1 30 61 2
48 32 53

PREGNANCY: Without exception, the most important period in the life of the unborn child. Uncontrolled habits, smoking, drinking alcoholic and "soft drink" beverages as well as cow's milk (particularly when pasteurized), and eat-

161

ing excessive quantities of concentrated starch, grain, and sugar foods on the part of the pregnant woman, all tend toward degeneracy or miner?' deficiency in the child. Raw vegetables and fruits, which are live organic foods, supplemented with an ample volume daily of fresh raw vegetables juices, as the regular daily diet have resulted in bright, healthy children as well as mothers. Try it! Read the whole chapter on CARROT JUICE.

PROLAPSUS: The falling of an organ from its normal position due to loss of tone in the nerve and muscular system as a result of improper diet. 61 2 30 40 15

PROSTATE TROUBLE: The result either of excess, or of a lack of vital live nourishment in the food for years past. 23 30 61 1 85

PSORIASIS: A group or colony of germs feeding on morbid matter and body waste in the system attempting to leave the body by way of the skin, thus creating an irritation. 61 30 15 1 2

PYELITIS: Inflammation in the region of the pelvis or the kidneys usually due to an excessive retention of uric acid in the system. 30 61 1 40 29 28 59

PYORRHEA: Inflammation of the gums and the loosening of the teeth because of the presence of excessive waste matter in the entire system, and the deficiency in the diet of live organic food. 61 1 2 30

PYROSIS (Heart-burn): Intense burning sensation, due to the presence of excessive uric acid or other morbid matter, resulting from the fermentation and putre- 30 61 29 40 59

162

faction of improper combinations of food.

QUINSY: Inflammation of the throat due to the presence of excessive body and food waste in the system. When an abscess forms, it is the localizing of waste matter in the region of the tonsils (which see). This has responded satisfactorily to detoxication (which also see).   61 30   2   1

RACHITIS (Rickets): Deficiency of organic calcium and other elements resulting in deformity, softness, or flexibility of the bones.   61   1 48 37   6 30 46

RENAL CALCULUS (Kidney Stones): Inorganic matter, principally the calcium in concentrated starches, forming concretions in the kidneys.   (in glass of hot water) 30 61 40 29 28 59 23

RHEUMATISM: Meat and meat products of any kind cannot be digested without an excessive accumulation of uric acid in the system. (Read the chapter on Carrot, Beet and Cucumber Juice). Retained in the body, this uric acid is absorbed into the muscles and sooner or later crystallizes. The sharp uric acid crystals are the cause of the pain in Rheumatism. (Read chapter on Protein in DIET & SALAD Book.)   23 30 61

RHINITIS: Inflammation of the nasal membrane principally due to the presence of excessive quantities of mucus in the sinus cavities.   61 30 40 11

SCARLET FEVER: The rebellion of the body against the accumulation of food waste and body waste in the system as a   30 61 68 47 66

163

result of eating too much cooked and not enough raw food and juices.

SCIATICA: Inflammation of the Sciatic nerve or surrounding muscle, usually due to the presence of excessive uric acid in the system.   30 61 40 28 / 29 59

SCLEROSIS: A hardening of any tissue of the body. (See also Multiple Sclerosis.)   61 62 32 30

SCROFULA: The formation of pus in the glands due to the presence of inorganic matter in the food eaten.   61 2 15 40 / 30

SCURVY: The result of an improperly balanced diet with insufficient organic nourishment.   61 15 2 30 / 29

SEXUAL DISEASES: Due to overindulgence leading to inflammation, and weakened organs due to lack of sufficient organic nourishment, resulting in disturbed functions, and the presence of morbid matter inviting the propagation of germs and infection.   61 30 2 15 / 40 29 28

SINUS TROUBLE: Usually due to excessive mucus resulting from excessive use of milk and frequently also of starches and sugars.   61 11 30 1

SLEEPLESSNESS: The result of excessive nervous tension and the improper elimination of waste from the body.   61 22 37 30

SMALLPOX: Excessive volumes of putrid waste matter in the body result in the propagation therein of the virulent germs responsible for this disease, which after the first burst of propagation leave the body by way of the pores of the skin. To   61 30 1 2 / 37 40 53 55

164

the informed vaccination against this disease is known to be not only of no value whatsoever, but a definite danger in its aftereffects. It has been declared that far more people have been crippled or otherwise incapacitated by the injection into their body of the putrid vaccine from diseased cattle, regularly used in vaccination, than have died from the disease. A body which is clean inside and out, and properly nourished with live organic food and fresh raw juices in abundance and variety, does not propagate this germ and is therefore immune to this disease.

STERILITY: A condition occasionally due to functional disorganization of the organism. As a general rule it is due to the lack of live, organic atoms in the food for years past, and the consequent accumulation of waste in the system.   61 30 1 2   29 40 48

SYPHILIS: The name given to the presence in the body of the Spirochaeta Pallida germ, when this germ finds the right kind of waste matter in the system on which it can thrive and propagate. This waste matter usually results from such foods as starch and meat products, and pasteurized milk.   61 30 66 62   51 46

THROMBOSIS: The result of the coagulation of a clot of blood obstructing a blood vessel because of the presence in the blood stream of starch molecules from breads, cereals, and other starches which are not soluble in water.   62 2 61 30

TONSILLITIS: The result of the overworking of the tonsils causing them to become inflamed. The tonsils are the first line of defense and their function is to control   61 30 1 2

165

the entrance into the body of too large an
army of germs when the waste matter in
the body accumulates too rapidly. In my
opinion, the removal of tonsils is analo-
gous to castration. It also affects the per-
sonality often transforming the child or
adult into a eunuch-like individual, and
females into slovenly, frigid characters. A
rapid degeneration of the body structure
has often been observed. (Reports by
Drs. I. & G. Calderoli of Bergamo, Italy:
"Il Sottosesso nei popoli senza tonsille,"
after having collected more than 30,000
of their case histories resulting from their
work in the Universities of Berlin and of
Vienna. (I have conferred personally
with Doctor Calderoli and can vouch for
the accuracy of their reports. Their collab-
orators were, among others, Doctors:
Passow, Killian, Halle, Jansen, Albrecht,
Gutzman, Hofer, Piehler, Marschik.)

TOXEMIA: Poisoning either as a result of   61 30 37 15
undue retention of body waste or of the   40
end-products of metabolism or digestion,
creating an over-acid condition.

TUBERCULOSIS: The result of excessive   61 45 1 30
mucus in the system causing the propaga-   2 11 37 40
tion of the tubercular germ, which by its   41
presence and mode of existence is destructive to the tissues in its proximity.
Cow's milk, both the raw and the pasteurized, is probably the most mucus-forming
food used by man, and such mucus is the
natural breeding food for such germs.
Probably more tuberculosis results from
using pasteurized milk than from any
other cause.

TUMORS   62 61 30 40
   in Brain   Growths due to a lack

in Bones   of sufficient organic
in Liver   elements and caused
in Uterus   by the excessive use
of concentrated inorganic foods, mostly
flour products. Contributing factors are
such destructive negative states of mind as
life-long resentments, anger, frustration,
etc.

TYPHOID: A condition due to the lack of   61 30 28 1
certain organic elements in the body, al-   37 6
lowing the propagation therein of germs
causing, by their presence, a mesenteric
fever.

ULCERS (chiefly gastric): A deficiency   61 1 30 5
disease caused by unhealthy tissue as a   37 6
result of eating incompatible combinations of food leaving fermentation and
putrefaction as their end-product. Can
also be attributed to excessive worry and
the other negative contributing factors
listed under the headings of CANCER
and TUMORS, which see.

UNDULANT FEVER: One of the several   61 30 20 22
means Nature adopts to burn up or incin-   23
erate waste matter in the system. In this
case the germ, active in breaking down
the waste, acts as a stoker—figuratively
speaking—raising the temperature of the
body at intervals, and sometimes continu-
ously. No waste—no fever! Undulant
fever germs thrive on pasteurized milk.

UREMIA: The presence of urea and other   30 61 29 40
urinary excretions in the blood.   59

URTICARIA (Hives): An excessively acid   61 2 30 15
condition of the body trying to become   1
normal by means of excretion through the
skin. (See Allergy.)

VARICOSE VEINS: The result of diets **61 2 30** 62
rich in concentrated starches and sugar 15
causing calcareous deposits to form in the
wall structure of the veins.

SOMETHING TO REMEMBER!

YOU now have the information you need to begin a completely NEW LIFE—if you have read this book carefully from beginning to end, as the Author sincerely hopes you have.

ACTION is the next step. You can read a good travel book and find a place you want to visit, but unless you save up the money for the trip and arrange for the most practical means of transportation, set a time of departure and GO, you will not have the actual experience of enjoying the trip as a reality.

It takes a lot of "GET UP AND GO" to make any basic changes in your way of living, particularly where it concerns your eating habits of a lifetime, which may all have been wrong.

Prevention is the intelligent approach, and ALL young people who are still well and healthy should read this book and put the principles into practice in their own lives, instead of waiting until they have developed ailments and discomforts which force them to do something about recovering their health.

We are receiving an ever increasing number of letters from very young people, some still in their teens and many in their early twenties who have read this book, and it has changed the entire course of their future life, and given them new goals and enthusiasm to attain them.

A lovely young couple wrote recently from California—"Dr. Walker, Thank you so much. We have been following your diet for the past six months and the changes it has made in our lives is remarkable. Our breast-fed baby is a joy in our home since I have changed my diet; all we feed him is avocados, apples and carrot juice, and he is bright and full of Nature's energy. God Bless you."

Another young man of 21 also wrote from California—"Dear Dr. Walker, I'm 21 years young and I'm a newcomer to the health movement. I started my change in diet almost one year ago. I am at this time almost practically on a raw food diet of fruits and vegetables. Occasionally I eat some cottage cheese (in a fruit salad) and once in a while some nuts. I gave up all starches (bread) and sugar, etc. I'm a seeker of life, and I believe in God, and I have faith in Nature's method of healing. Also I don't smoke pot—I've already been through the drug scene, and that's why I thank God that I was lucky enough to see the light of truth— 'life through natural living.' "

* * *

Whether you are 8 or 80, the contents of this book are meant for YOU.

Health is the indisputable foundation for the satisfaction of life, for success, socially and financially.

God blessed you with a body which in its natural functions is a MIRACLE—what are you doing with it??

GET INFORMED—THEN ACT—for no matter what the condition of your body is today, it CAN BE CHANGED.

With vibrant health and energy, the mind can function clearly, and problems and difficulties will only be challenges to meet and overcome.

YOU have a destiny to be fulfilled—GET INFORMED!!!

BE PREPARED!!!

ACT!!!

If anything in this book has given you pleasure, benefit or happiness, write it down and let us know about it. It matters not whether this is your book or if it is loaned to you. This is the only way we can know that our work has been profitable to the reader.

We will appreciate it, even though it is only a postcard with one or two words and your name and address on it.

(Please note that we have no facilities for answering letters requesting HEALTH information.)

NORWALK PRESS, Publishers
P. O. Box 13206, Phoenix, Arizona
85002

INDEX